Fault Lines
Economic Terrain

MW00723924

"*Fault Lines in China's Economic Terrain*...should be of compelling interest to government officials and scholars....timely, carefully researched, and well-written, ...a significant contribution [to] this vital issue."

—**William Perry**
*Senior Fellow, Hoover Institution, and Professor of Engineering
and International Studies, Stanford University;
former Secretary of Defense*

"...raise[s] some fascinating situations that China will likely encounter in the coming decade. China 'buffs' will not want to miss this thoughtful exposition of the challenges ahead."

—**John Raisian**
Director, Hoover Institution, Stanford University

"Based on its 25-year record of success, the Chinese economy might be expected to soar into the far future. This imaginative book addresses an array of possible disruptive events....a usefully sober alternative to the familiar, rosy scenario."

—**Henry Rowen**
*Senior Fellow, Hoover Institution, and Professor of Public Policy
and Management Emeritus, Stanford University*

"...a signal contribution to those pondering China's economic future."

—**James Sasser**
*former U.S. Ambassador to China
and former U.S. Senator from Tennessee*

"China has astounded the world with a record of near double-digit growth for over two decades.... This analytically sophisticated assessment of eight 'fault lines' in China's current economic circumstances highlights the dangers.... an important corrective to the view that China can sustain an annual growth rate of 7% or more without risk of setbacks that could be socially or politically destabilizing."

—**Richard Solomon**
*President, United States Institute of Peace;
former Assistant Secretary of State for East Asian and Pacific Affairs*

Fault Lines in China's Economic Terrain

Charles Wolf, Jr., K.C. Yeh, Benjamin Zycher,
Nicholas Eberstadt, Sung-Ho Lee

Prepared for the Office of Net Assessment, Department of Defense, and the Smith Richardson Foundation
Approved for public release; distribution unlimited

RAND

National Defense Research Institute

The research described in this report was sponsored jointly by the Office of Net Assessment in the Department of Defense and the Smith Richardson Foundation. The research was conducted in RAND's National Defense Research Institute, a federally funded research and development center supported by the Office of the Secretary of Defense, the Joint Staff, the unified commands, and the defense agencies under Contract DASW01-01-C-0004.

Library of Congress Cataloging-in-Publication Data

Fault lines in China's economic terrain / Charles Wolf ... [et al.].
   p. cm.
   "MR-1686."
   ISBN 0-8330-3344-1 (pbk.)
   1. China—Economic conditions—2000- 2. China—Social conditions—2000-
3. Public health—China. I. Wolf, Charles, 1924–

HC427.95.F37 2003
330.951—dc21

                                          2003002047

RAND is a nonprofit institution that helps improve policy and decisionmaking through research and analysis. RAND® is a registered trademark. RAND's publications do not necessarily reflect the opinions or policies of its research sponsors.

Cover design by Maritta Tapanainen

Published 2003 by RAND
1700 Main Street, P.O. Box 2138, Santa Monica, CA 90407-2138
1200 South Hayes Street, Arlington, VA 22202-5050
201 North Craig Street, Suite 202, Pittsburgh, PA 15213-1516
RAND URL: http://www.rand.org/
To order RAND documents or to obtain additional information,
contact Distribution Services: Telephone: (310) 451-7002;
Fax: (310) 451-6915; Email: order@rand.org

The focus of this research is the potential adversities or fault lines (the terms are used synonymously) facing China's economy and affecting its prospects for sustaining high growth through the coming decade. Thus, we deliberately concentrate on what might go seriously awry in the economy and, in the process, slow or even reverse China's double-digit growth rates in the 1980s and high single-digit growth in the 1990s and the early part of the 21st century.

This book is the product of a project jointly sponsored by the Office of Net Assessment in the Department of Defense and the Smith Richardson Foundation. Their sponsorship was based on a mutual understanding that their joint support would enable the work to be expanded beyond what would have been possible if funding were confined to one sponsor alone.

The project was implemented through RAND's National Defense Research Institute (NDRI), a federally funded research and development center sponsored by the Office of the Secretary of Defense, the Joint Staff, the unified commands, and the defense agencies.

The book should be of interest and use to those in the policy community and the academic community concerned with China and with the economic and security environment in the Asia-Pacific region.

CONTENTS

FIGURES

TABLES

What are the major challenges, fault lines, and potential adversities (these terms are used synonymously) that China's economic development will encounter over the next decade?[1] How severely will China's overall economic performance be affected if these adversities occur separately or in clusters? This book addresses these key questions. We deliberately concentrate on what might go seriously awry in the economy and, in the process, slow or even reverse China's double-digit growth rates in the 1980s and high single-digit growth in the 1990s and the early part of the 21st century. We do not devote equivalent attention to the means by which China might prevent, mitigate, or remedy these adversities. Nor do we consider the potential sources of resilience and strength that could offset or absorb these adversities.

This asymmetry is deliberate. Its intent is to provide a countervailing perspective to what has been a generally prevailing consensus, with a few notable exceptions, that China's economy will be able to sustain high rates of economic growth for the indefinite future.

In considering what might go seriously wrong in the Chinese economy, we have focused on eight domains, summarized below. For each, we estimate a "bottom line" in terms of expected effects on China's annual growth rate over the next decade, drawing on a variety of methods, models, and judgments to make these estimates.

---

[1]In a few instances (for example, Chapter Four deals with epidemic disease, and Chapter Five deals with water resources), the consequences of adverse scenarios are evaluated through 2025.

Most of the problems that we examine are ones that China has confronted in the past and, notwithstanding, has managed with sufficient success to sustain high rates of economic growth. Consequently, our focus is on whether and by how much these adversities might be worsened in the future, and with what effects.

Our principal findings together with estimates about the corresponding bottom lines can be summarized as follows.

UNEMPLOYMENT, POVERTY, AND SOCIAL UNREST

Open and disguised unemployment in China amounts to about 23 percent of the total labor force, or approximately 170 million. Recent and prospective increases in unemployment have been principally due to population increases in the 1980s and the privatization and downsizing of the often inefficient, loss-incurring state-owned enterprises. China's efforts to comply with its World Trade Organization (WTO) commitments may engender more unemployment. Rural poverty has led to increased income inequality between rural and urban areas, rural-to-urban migration, rising urban unemployment, and social unrest.

Potential worsening of these adversities may cause a reduction between 0.3 and 0.8 percent in China's annual growth rate in the coming decade as a result of lower factor productivity, lower savings, and reduced capital formation.

ECONOMIC EFFECTS OF CORRUPTION

To calibrate corruption in China and to link it to China's expected economic performance, we have drawn on two established indices of corruption and their association with differing quintile positions in annual economic growth rates of the various countries included in the indices. Were corrupt practices in China to increase—as a result of plausible though not demonstrable recent trends—the result would be to lower China's position in the quintile distribution linking economic growth with the prevalence of corrupt practices.

The result of this adverse shift would be a reduction of about 0.5 percent in China's expected annual growth rate.

HIV/AIDS AND EPIDEMIC DISEASE

Estimates by the United Nations and other sources place the prevalence of HIV/AIDS in China between 600,000 and 1.3 million, with an approximate annual rate of increase between 20 and 30 percent. To analyze the effects of possible further disease spread, several scenarios are simulated, which include varying estimates of the costs of therapy, the effects of disease on factor productivity, and the effects on per-capita output. The bottom-line estimate for the "intermediate" rather than "pessimistic" scenarios is a trajectory of annual deaths from HIV/AIDS in China between 1.7 and 2.7 million in the second decade of the 21st century, cumulating by 2020 to over 20 million casualties and associated with annual reductions in gross domestic product (GDP) growth between 1.8 and 2.2 percent in the period 2002 to 2015.

WATER RESOURCES AND POLLUTION

China is beset by a perennial maldistribution of natural water supplies. The North China plain, with over a third of China's population and at least an equivalent share of its GDP, has only 7.5 percent of the naturally available water resources. Subsurface aquifers in North China are near exhaustion, and pollution discharges from industrial and other sources further aggravate the shortage of water for consumers and industry. By contrast, South China normally has an abundance of natural water supplies, sometimes leading to serious floods. The dilemma this poses for China's policymakers is whether to push for capital-intensive water-transfer projects from south to north, or to emphasize recycling as well as conservation of water supplies in the north, or to pursue a combination of these alternatives. This key allocation issue is further complicated by political considerations relating to the relative influence of provinces in the north and south.

We examine several different scenarios involving different combinations of water-transfer projects and recycling/conservation efforts intended to reduce the stringencies in water resource availability in the north. For various reasons, nonoptimal policy decisions and resource allocations might be pursued. A plausible but adverse scenario would result in a reduction in China's annual GDP growth between 1.5 and 1.9 percent in the ensuing decade.

ENERGY CONSUMPTION AND PRICES

One risk posed for China's sustained high growth rate is the availability of oil and natural gas supplies at what might be sharply increased world energy prices. Price changes constitute the main risk, rather than China's shift from being a net exporter of oil in the early 1990s to a situation in which nearly half of its oil and nearly a fifth of its natural gas consumption are derived from imports.

To analyze this potential adversity, we consider several scenarios in which there is a drastic contraction in global oil supplies by about 25 percent lasting for a decade (2005–2015). The several scenarios consider a range of plausible demand elasticities, together with allowance for increased energy efficiency, resulting in a conservative estimate of increased global oil prices by as much as threefold.

The resulting bottom-line effect on China's annual growth rate stemming from a "moderately severe" scenario during the period 2005–2015 would be an average diminution between 1.2 and 1.4 percent.

FRAGILITY OF THE FINANCIAL SYSTEM AND STATE-OWNED ENTERPRISES

One salient indicator of the fragility of China's state-dominated financial institutions is the extraordinarily high rate of nonperforming loans (NPLs) on the balance sheets of the four major state banks. NPLs have risen and continue to rise as a result of accumulated "policy lending" from the state banks to loss-incurring state-owned enterprises. Estimates of total NPLs cover an enormous range, between 9 percent and 60 percent of China's GDP: The correct figure is more likely to be at the upper end of this range.

Under various plausible circumstances, China could experience a panic "run" of withdrawals from the state banks, large-scale capital flight, a significant reduction in savings, and a sharp decline in capital formation. The ensuing financial crisis and credit squeeze could plausibly reduce total factor productivity by 0.3 percent, with an accompanying reduction in the annual rates of growth of capital stock and of employment that would collectively lower annual GDP growth by 0.5 to 1.0 percent.

POSSIBLE SHRINKAGE OF FOREIGN DIRECT INVESTMENT

Between 1985 and 2001, foreign direct investment (FDI) in China rose from an annual rate of about $2 billion to over $40 billion in 2001, in constant 1995 dollars. Analysts both within and outside China agree that FDI has been of considerable importance and has had leveraging effects for China's high rates of real economic growth, although there is considerable disagreement about the mechanisms that account for these leveraging effects.

High rates of FDI may well continue in the future, but there are also not implausible circumstances under which this FDI might severely contract. These adverse circumstances include both possible *internal* developments (such as tensions accompanying the leadership succession, the possibility of internal financial crisis, inconvertibility of the renminbi, and slow implementation of China's WTO pledges), as well as possible *external* developments (such as improvements in the economic infrastructure and investment climate in other competing countries and regions in Eastern Europe, Russia, India, and elsewhere). To a greater extent than in the past, future FDI in China will depend critically on the comparative risk-adjusted, after-tax return on investment in China compared with that of other countries.

Based on very rough assumptions and using three plausible but admittedly imprecise methods, our preliminary calculations suggest that a sustained reduction of $10 billion a year in FDI may be associated with an expected reduction in China's annual GDP growth between 0.6 and 1.6 percent.

TAIWAN AND OTHER POTENTIAL CONFLICTS

The status quo in the perennially troubled relationship between China and Taiwan entails major benefits for the People's Republic of China (PRC), Taiwan, and the United States. However, there are also significant risks and tensions associated with the status quo. It is not inconceivable that these tensions might erupt into possible conflict between the PRC and Taiwan.

We consider one scenario involving escalation from what Beijing might view as provocation by Taiwan, a blockade imposed by the PRC in response, tangible though limited coercive force to effectuate the blockade, and the resulting effects on China's stock markets, exchange rates, and reallocations of resources to military spending, with ensuing reductions in the rate of growth of the civil capital stock and in total factor productivity.

The bottom line of these adverse developments would be a decline in China's annual rate of economic growth, conservatively estimated at 1.0–1.3 percent.

Table S.1 summarizes our rough estimates of the potential effects on China's annual real economic growth that could ensue from each of the several adversities or fault lines, were they to occur separately on a one-at-a-time basis.[2]

Table S.1

Impacts on China's Growth Arising from Separate Fault Lines, 2005–2015 (Preliminary)

Type of Setback	Separate Effects Diminishing China's Economic Performance (percentage/year)
Unemployment, poverty, social unrest	0.3–0.8
Economic effects of corruption	0.5
HIV/AIDS and epidemic disease	1.8–2.2
Water resources and pollution	1.5–1.9
Energy consumption and prices	1.2–1.4
Fragility of the financial system and state-owned enterprises	0.5–1.0
Possible shrinkage of foreign direct investment	0.6–1.6
Taiwan and other potential conflicts	1.0–1.3

---

[2]These results beg the question of how long each of these adverse effects would endure without inducing remedial efforts or, failing to induce them, having "contagion" effects on the other adversities.

The probability that none of these individual setbacks will occur is low, while the probability that all will occur is still lower. Were all of them to occur, our estimates indicate that China's growth would be reduced between 7.4 and 10.7 percent annually, thus registering negative numbers for China's economic performance as a whole. While the probability that all will occur is very low, the probability that several will ensue is higher than their joint probabilities would normally imply. The reason for this multiplication of effect is that their individual probabilities are not independent of one another; the occurrence of one or two will raise the probability that others will ensue. Because of these interdependencies, it is highly likely that several of the separate adversities would tend to cluster if any one of them occurs. As examples: an internal financial crisis would have serious negative consequences for the relative attractiveness of foreign investment in China, conducing to shrinkage of FDI; epidemic disease would intensify water pollution problems and would discourage foreign investment.

Table S.2 suggests some of the key interdependencies among the several fault lines we have discussed.

Table S.2

Interdependencies Among Fault Lines

Consequence \\ Cause	Unemployment, poverty, and social unrest	Economic effects of corruption	HIV/AIDS and epidemic disease	Water resources and pollution	Energy consumption and prices	Fragility of the financial system and state-owned enterprises	Possible shrinkage of foreign direct investment	Taiwan and other potential conflicts
Unemployment, poverty, and social unrest	▨	✔	✔	✔	✔	✔		
Economic effects of corruption	✔	▨				✔	✔	
HIV/AIDS and epidemic disease	✔		▨	✔	✔			
Water resources and pollution	✔		✔	▨	✔			
Energy consumption and prices	✔				▨			
Fragility of the financial system and state-owned enterprises	✔	✔	✔			▨	✔	✔
Possible shrinkage of foreign direct investment	✔	✔	✔			✔	▨	✔
Taiwan and other potential conflicts								▨

RAND*MR1686T-S.2*

NOTE: ✔ indicates where a fault line (cause/column heading) is likely to affect the occurrence and/or severity of another (consequence/row heading).

ACKNOWLEDGMENTS

The authors are pleased to acknowledge the valuable comments we received on an earlier version of this book from Henry Rowen at Stanford University, RAND colleague Steven Popper, and David Epstein in the Department of Defense. While we have taken their comments into account in revising the book, none of them bears responsibility for any of the judgments or estimates we have made.

We also wish to acknowledge the effort and assistance we have received from Leah Borges in assembling and formatting the draft text, and from Christina Pitcher in editing and integrating the complex elements of the entire manuscript.

ACRONYMS AND ABBREVIATIONS

ABC	Agricultural Bank of China
AFP	American Foreign Press
AWSJ	*Asian Wall Street Journal*
BOC	Bank of China
Btu	British thermal unit
CAS	Chinese Academy of Sciences
CASS	Chinese Academy of Social Sciences
CBC	Construction Bank of China
CCP	Chinese Communist Party
CD	*China Daily*, Beijing
CDC	U.S. Centers for Disease Control and Prevention
CDN	*Chinese Daily News*, Los Angeles
CITIC	China International Trust and Investment Corporation
CLA	China Labor Association
COD	chemical oxygen demand
DALY	disability adjusted life year
DRC	Development Research Center, State Council
EIA	Energy Information Administration

FBIS	Foreign Broadcast Information Service
FDI	foreign direct investment
GDP	gross domestic product
ha	hectare
HAART	Highly Active Anti-Retroviral Therapy
ICBC	Industrial and Commercial Bank of China
IMF	International Monetary Fund
ITC	investment and trust company
IV	intravenous
l/c/d	liters per capita per day
MOL	Ministry of Labor
MOLS	Ministry of Labor and Social Security
NPL	nonperforming loan
OECD	Organisation for Economic Co-operation and Development
PBC	People's Bank of China
PPP	purchasing power parity
PRC	People's Republic of China
RMB	renminbi (People's currency, used synonymously with "yuan," which is the traditional designation of China's currency)
SA	*Statistical Abstract*
SCMP	*South China Morning Post*, Hong Kong
SLOCs	sea lines of communications
SOE	state-owned enterprise
SSB	State Statistical Bureau
SY	*Statistical Yearbook*
TFP	total factor productivity

TKP	*Ta kung pao*, Hong Kong
UNAIDS	Joint United Nations Programme on HIV/AIDS
WDR	World Bank, *World Development Report*
WHO	World Health Organization
WHP	*Wen hui pao*, Hong Kong
WRI	World Resource Institute
WSJ	*The Wall Street Journal*
WTO	World Trade Organization

Chapter One

POTENTIAL ADVERSITIES CONFRONTING CHINA'S CONTINUED ECONOMIC GROWTH

Widely divergent views about China's future are prevalent among policymakers, politicians, pundits, business people, analysts, and academics. Prominent among the questions on which their views diverge are the following:

1. At what rates and for how long will China continue its rapid economic growth of the past two decades?[1]

2. What are the major challenges, fault lines, and potential adversities (the terms are used synonymously in this study) that China's economic development will encounter in the next decade, and how much of an impact on its economic performance will these have if they occur separately or in clusters?

3. How will the rate of China's economic growth affect the pace and content of its military modernization?[2]

---

[1]The U.S.-China Security Review Commission in its hearings and final report in 2002 generally displayed a consensus view that high rates of economic growth in China would continue for the foreseeable future. See *Compilation of Hearings Held Before the U.S.-China Security Review Commission, 107th Congress First and Second Sessions, Fiscal Years 2001 and 2002*, U.S. Government Printing Office, Washington, D.C., 2002; also available from U.S.-China Security Review Commission, www.uscc.gov. For a sharply divergent although distinctly minority view among putative experts on China, see Gordon Chang, *The Coming Collapse of China*, Random House, New York, 2001.

[2]The wide range of differing views on both questions 3 and 4 are evident in the report of the U.S.-China Security Review Commission, see *Report to Congress of the U.S.-China Security Review Commission—The National Security Implications of the Economic Relationship Between the United States and China*, July 2002, especially pp. 167–

4. Is China's sustained rapid growth beneficial or harmful to U.S. national economic and security interests?[3]

These questions are large, complex, and interrelated. From a U.S. policy perspective, the answer to question 4, if it were convincing, would constitute a sort of "bottom line." Whether continued high growth is beneficial to U.S. interests depends in considerable measure on whether one adheres to the view that political pluralism, democratization, and benign rather than aggressive Chinese foreign and defense policy are helped, hindered, or not affected by high rather than low rates of growth. Moreover, embedded in this question are other questions relating to the probabilities associated with these outcomes, and how these probabilities would be affected by high rather than low growth. Even strong advocates of the positive, benign view of the effect of economic growth would not—or at least *should not*—impute certainty to the connective links between economic and political change. The phenomena and the linkages among them are, as Winston Churchill once observed about the Soviet Union's behavior, "a riddle wrapped in a mystery inside an enigma."

In this study of aspects of China's future, we focus principally on the second question mentioned above: What are the major potential adversities, or fault lines, confronting China's economic development over the next decade, and how much would these adversities affect China's economic performance? We do not address directly the first question of "how long," or indeed "whether," China will sustain high growth. Although inferences with respect to answering question 1 might be drawn from the data and analysis provided in our effort to answer question 2, these inferences would not be warranted. The

---

178 on The Defense Budget and China's Military Economy. Although the commission acknowledges the possibly benign aspects of China's continued economic growth, the predominant view conveyed by the report places more emphasis on the malign and possibly threatening facets of this growth. For example, note the following statement issued by commission member and former president of the U.S. steel workers George Becker when the report was published:

> Unless our country changes course, the tragic fact that China's resurgence is being financed by U.S. firms at the expense of American workers will one day be seen as the first stage in China's strategy of asserting its industrial preeminence over us (Office of Commissioner Becker, Press Release, July 15, 2002).

[3]U.S.-China Security Review Commission, especially pp. 1–2, 4–5.

reason for avoiding such inferences is that we have not attempted to assess the opportunities, instruments, and policies that China might be able to utilize to sustain its growth by offsetting the serious "adversities" that are the focus of this study. Thus, we do not address the sources of resilience and strength as possible counters to Chinese economic fault lines—countervailing elements that include, for example, the expanded resources generated by China's rapid and sustained economic growth, which provide additional means for addressing and redressing the adversities discussed in this study.

This asymmetry is deliberate. Its intent is to provide a countervailing perspective to what has been a generally prevailing consensus—with a few notable exceptions—among policymakers, businessmen, and scholars both within and outside China: namely, that China's economy will be able to sustain high rates of economic growth for the indefinite future. This consensus is, for example, reflected in analyses and forecasts by the World Bank, the Organisation for Economic Co-Operation and Development (OECD), the Institute for International Economics, and in the hearings and final report of the U.S.-China Security Review Commission.[4]

In considering what might go seriously wrong in the Chinese economy, we have focused on eight domains, described in Chapters Two–Nine. For each of them, we have tried to arrive at a bottom line in terms of their respective effects on China's annual growth rate should each of these adversities occur. To arrive at each bottom line, we have used the aggregate growth model employed in other RAND work on the Chinese and other Asian economies (Wolf et al., 2000) or through other methods and calculations tailored to and described in each of the eight separate chapters.

The adversities that may confront China over the next decade cover a wide range of possibilities. These may be categorized as *institutional and structural* (e.g., rural and urban unemployment, poverty, and corruption), *sectoral* (e.g., HIV/AIDS and epidemic disease, water resources and pollution, and energy), *financial* (e.g., internal financial crisis and shrinkage of foreign direct investment), and *security* (e.g.,

---

[4]See reference reports, memoranda, and other papers published by these organizations.

military tension and conflict in the Taiwan Strait and other parts of the Asia-Pacific region).

China has confronted in the past two decades five of the eight fault lines that we consider (unemployment, corruption, water resources problems, HIV/AIDS, and financial fragility) and, nonetheless, has sustained high rates of economic growth. Hence, in assessing the potential impact on China's future economic performance of these fault lines, our focus is on whether, why, and by how much their intensities may increase—that is, on *changes*, rather than on the prevailing *levels* of each fault line. For the other three fault lines that have not previously occurred or recurred—oil price shock, foreign direct investment (FDI) shrinkage, and serious military conflicts—we consider the circumstances under which they arise and their resulting economic effects.

While the potential adversities that we address are formidable, they are by no means an exhaustive list. For example, we do not address the possibility of internal political strife that might ensue in the leadership succession and transition from the *so-called* 4th-generation leadership (i.e., Jiang Zemin and his septuagenarian associates) to the 3rd-generation leadership (Hu Jintao and his sexagenarian associates). Nor do we address the effects of a possible intensification of economic disparities between the relatively rich eastern provinces and the impoverished western ones. And we do not consider the possibility that internal economic barriers among China's 37 provinces and special administrative regions might grow, thereby obstructing the operation of markets and hindering efficient resource allocation. While these omissions are touched on in several of the chapters, they are not addressed in detail. Thus, what we cover is a selective, rather than exhaustive, set of adversities.

Figure 1.1 depicts these adversities and how each would affect China's economic performance.

Tier IV of Figure 1.1 shows the numerous fault lines that already loom large among the problems that China faces, and that may loom even larger in the future. The successive chapters focus on empirical data to quantify each of the selected adversities. In most cases, we

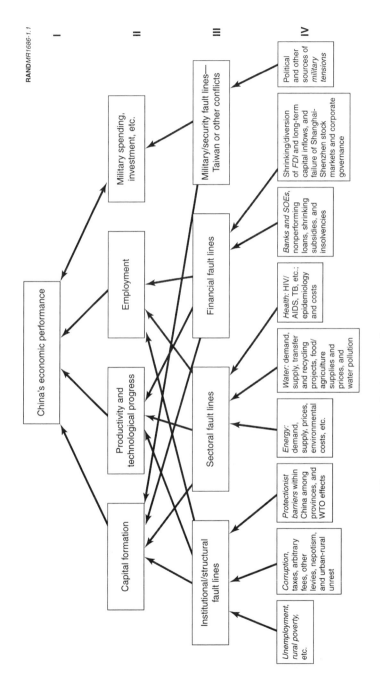

Figure 1.1—Fault Lines in China's Economic Terrain

use "severe" rather than "worst-case" scenarios to assess quantitatively the separate consequences that would follow from, respectively, high unemployment and rural poverty, the economic costs of corruption, water resource problems and pollution, HIV/AIDS and epidemic disease, increased energy prices, possible internal financial crisis, a shrinkage of foreign direct investment, and security tensions in the Taiwan Strait and elsewhere in the region.

Tier III of Figure 1.1 provides a rough categorization of these separate fault lines in terms of the institutional, sectoral, financial, and security categories mentioned above.

Tier II summarizes the standard model that we sometimes use in this study and have used in prior studies[5] to evaluate the separate effects on China's aggregate economic performance (Tier I) that would ensue from each of these adversities. In evaluating the effects on economic growth, we apply the standard model in several instances (e.g., to assess the effects of increased unemployment, water and pollution difficulties, financial crisis, and possible military conflict in the Taiwan Strait). For several other adversities, we use regression models, alternative scenarios, and other methods described in the corresponding chapters to derive rough estimates of potential effects on China's economic growth.

A possible bias is introduced into our analysis because the method we use assesses the effects of each adversity separately from the effects of others. This "one-at-a-time" procedure implies that the probabilities of their occurrence are independent of one another, when in fact many of them are interdependent. Although we do not assign prior probabilities to each of the adversities, it can be inferred that the probability that *none* of them will occur is low, and the probability that *all* will occur is still lower.[6] However, the probability that several will occur is higher than their joint probabilities would normally imply, because of their interdependence. For example, it is rea-

---

[5]See Wolf et al., 2000, especially Appendix A, where the standard model is explained in detail.

[6]This assertion is based on the arguable but reasonable assumption that each of the separate adversities has a prior probability associated with it of less than 0.5—say, between 0.1 and 0.2.

sonable to presume that rural and urban unemployment, poverty, and the incidence of HIV/AIDS and other epidemic diseases will tend to cluster—poverty is likely to be associated with higher incidence of epidemic disease, and disease is likely to aggravate poverty. There is a similar linkage between possible internal financial crisis and the shrinkage of foreign direct investment. Furthermore, the prior probabilities of internal financial crisis and shrinkage of foreign direct investment would be significantly increased if military tensions or conflicts occurred in the Taiwan Strait.

In sum, the adversities that we address in the body of this book are more likely to occur in clusters of interrelated and hence interdependent adversities, rather than separately in a one-at-a-time mode.

The eight fault lines that we address are grouped into three parts: Part I, China's Institutional and Structural Fault Lines (Chapter Two, Massive Unemployment and Rural Poverty, Chapter Three, Economic Effects of Corruption); Part II, Sectoral Fault Lines (Chapter Four, Epidemic Disease: A Wild Card in China's Economic Future? Chapter Five, Water Resources and Pollution, and Chapter Six, GDP Effects of an Energy Price Shock); Part III, Financial Fault Lines (Chapter Seven, China's Fragile Financial System and the State-Owned Enterprises, Chapter Eight, Possible Shrinkage of Foreign Capital Inflows); and Part IV, Security Fault Lines (Chapter Nine, Taiwan and Other Potential Conflicts).

Finally, Chapter Ten summarizes the principal findings of the preceding chapters and presents our conclusions. These conclusions can be summarized at a very general level as follows: Each of the potential adversities that we have examined entails a consequential risk of reducing the very high, single-digit growth of real gross domestic product (GDP) that China has sustained over the past 20 years. Moreover, if these adversities occur in clusters that reflect their interrelationships and interdependencies, China's economic picture would indeed become dark. The following chapters provide the data and analysis that lead to this broad conclusion.

PART I

CHINA'S INSTITUTIONAL AND STRUCTURAL FAULT LINES

Chapter Two

MASSIVE UNEMPLOYMENT AND RURAL POVERTY

This chapter reviews the current status and recent trends in unemployment and rural poverty in China and discusses how they might affect economic growth should conditions deteriorate in the next decade.

We define unemployment to include both open and disguised unemployment. Open unemployment refers to persons who are 16 years of age or over, are capable of working, and are actively seeking employment, but who have not been able to find employment. Disguised unemployment is loosely defined to include those whose removal from the workforce would have virtually no effect on output, assuming no change in production techniques or in the supply of other factors, but allowing organizational changes if necessary.[1] The reason for including the disguised unemployed in our definition is

---

[1]Disguised unemployment includes those who work "full time" but whose labor input per unit of time falls short of some standard because of work sharing. For example, if the standard is that three workers can harvest one acre of rice in one day, and if five workers do the same job over the same period of time, each putting in a full day's work though at a more leisurely pace, then, by our definition, two persons fall into the category of disguised unemployment. They all work full time but are not full-time equivalent workers in the strict sense. Nor are they part-time workers. The conceptual and measurement problems involving disguised unemployment are many. See Nurkse, 1953; Kao, Anschel, and Eicher, 1964; Myrdal, 1968; Sen, 1975; and Bhaduri, 1989. The controversy need not detain us here. That there is disguised unemployment in rural China is evidenced by findings of rural surveys and by the 30 some million peasants flooding the coastal cities looking for work in the 1990s, while agricultural output continued to grow without significant technological changes. See Cook, 1999; Development Research Center (DRC), 1994; and Fan and Hou, 2000. In the urban areas, a survey by the International Labor Office found an urban hidden unemployment rate of 18.8 percent in 1995 (Yang, 1997, p. 48).

that they are different from the openly unemployed only in form. In the current transition to a market-oriented economy, the disguised unemployed are steadily coming to the surface, and their effects on resource allocation and social stability are no less consequential than those of the openly unemployed.

Table 2.1 presents a rough estimate of unemployment in China in 1999.[2] For convenience of discussion, six categories of unemployment are distinguished. The first group, open urban unemployment, refers to unemployed urban residents, whether or not they have registered with the local labor office.[3] The second group comprises deactivated (xia-gang, or literally, "off-posts") workers and employees who are seeking reemployment.[4] A third group consists of the workers and employees in defunct enterprises, which have not yet gone bankrupt but have suspended operations. A fourth category includes unemployed persons in urban areas that do not fall into the officially defined urban unemployed. They include such persons as migrant workers from rural areas, underage youths, retirees, and individual (self-employed) workers who are out of work. The fifth category is the redundant workers in urban enterprises and organizations who have not yet been laid off. Sixth, there are the hidden unemployed in the rural areas.

---

[2]It should be noted that these estimates are at best informed guesses because of the lack of reliable data. Available estimates of China's unemployment vary widely because of differences in definition, sources, and methods. For example, estimates of total unemployment in 1995 range from 167 to 225 million. See Beijing *Xinhua,* March 1, 1995, reported in Foreign Broadcast Information Service, CHI-95-040, March 1, 1995, p. 41; *Wen hui pao* (WHP), January 3, 1995. Another example is that the Ministry of Labor estimates the urban hidden unemployment rate at 10–12 percent, compared to the 25 percent estimated by the State Planning Commission (Yang, 1997, p. 48).

[3]These estimates are from surveys by the State Statistical Bureau (SSB) and are different from official statistics of unemployment that cover only the registered unemployed urban residents (*Statistical Yearbook* [SY] 93, p. 140). Thus, the SSB estimate of 2.9 percent in 1995 is distinctly lower than the 4.5 percent urban unemployment based on survey data, which presumably include those not registered (SSB and Ministry of Labor and Social Security [MOLS], 2001, p. 67; Yang, 1997, p. 219). For this reason, it would be misleading to compare China's official unemployment rate with those of other countries as both the SSB and the World Bank did in SY 97, p. 884, and World Bank, 2001a, p. 56.

[4]The deactivated workers are those who have been laid off but who still maintain "labor relationships" with their work units (SSB and MOLS, 2001, p. 571).

Table 2.1

Unemployment, 1999

Unemployment	Total (millions)	Composition (%)	Unemployment Rate (%)
Urban, open	30.5	18.1	10.0
SSB survey data	14.0	8.3	—
Deactivated	9.4	5.6	—
Defunct units	6.0	3.6	—
Migrant workers	1.1	0.6	—
Urban, disguised	13.0	7.7	6.2
Rural, disguised	125.0	74.2	25.2
Total	168.5	100.0	22.9

SOURCES: Following the methodology used by the SSB in SSB and Ministry of Labor (MOL), 1997, p. 3, we derive the urban open unemployment (SSB survey data) by deducting total employment from economically active persons given in SY 00, p. 116. Estimates of deactivated urban workers and the migrant workers are taken from Hu, 2001a. Yang, 1997, p. 27, reported that unemployed workers in urban enterprises that had stopped or virtually stopped operations have remained at the level of 6 million since 1989. We assume the same level of defunct units in 1999. The urban disguised unemployment is derived as a residual, by deducting the total that have been deactivated since 1995, 20 million estimated in Chinese Academy of Sciences (CAS), 1998, p. 104, from the total redundant workers and employees, 33 million, given in Yang, 1997, pp. 75–76. Rural disguised unemployment is the midpoint of the range of estimates by the State Planning Commission in Zeng, 1999, p. 524, and the World Bank reported in *Chinese Daily News* (CDN), July 25, 1999. For total employment used to calculate unemployment rates, 210.1 and 495.7 million in urban and rural areas, respectively, see SY 00, pp. 118–119.

NOTE: "—" = not available.

An unemployment rate of 23 percent is high by any standards. The situation could remain severe and even worsen in the next decade, because of three distinct trends in the 1990s that could continue into the 2000s. First, despite an acceleration of GDP growth, from 9.3 percent per year during 1980–1990 to 10.1 percent during 1990–2000, the growth of employment fell markedly, from 4.2 percent in the 1980s to 1.1 percent in the 1990s (SY 01, pp. 52, 108). In short, there had been a sharp drop in the employment elasticity of output in the 1990s as compared to the preceding decade. Second, closely related to the decline in employment elasticity is the slowdown in the growth of employment in the major labor-absorbing sectors in the 1990s. For example, average annual growth of nonagricultural employment dropped from 6.8 percent in 1980–1990 to 3.4 percent in 1990–2000. Within the nonagricultural sector, growth of employment in the nonstate subsector fell from 11.2 to 6.2 percent; that of rural enterprises, from 11.9 to 3.3 percent; that of construction, from 9.3 to 3.9 percent; and that of services, from 7.9 to 5.2 percent, over the two periods, respectively (SY 01, pp. 108, 110–112). Third, the annual growth of total employment during 1980–1990, 4.2 percent, far exceeded that for the working-age population (population in the age group of 15–64 years, a proxy for labor supply)—2.3 percent over the same period. In contrast, the average annual growth of employment during 1990–2000, 1.1 percent, lagged behind the growth of the working-age population, 15 percent, over the same period.[5]

The trends in the 1990s could continue into the next decade, in part because of a possible slowdown in GDP growth, and in part because the growth of the working-age population could remain at about the same pace as in the last decade. In the 1990s, GDP growth has already been slowing, from 12 percent per year during 1990–1995 to 8.3 percent during 1995–2000 (SY 01, p. 52). Economic projections by the World Bank and the Chinese Academy of Social Sciences show a declining trend continuing into the next decade.[6] If that should occur, employment growth would probably fall as well. Meanwhile, continued population growth in the 1980s and 1990s will have an echo effect of increasing the working-age population during the 2000s. According to one estimate, the annual growth of the working-age population will drop only slightly, from 1.5 percent during 1990–2000 to 1.4 percent during 2000–2010 (SA 01, p. 36; Lin and Zhai, 1996, p. 23). Given the divergent trends in the growth of employment and the working-age population, and the huge current backlog of unemployment, a worsening of the situation is a distinct possibility.

Closely related to unemployment is the problem of rural poverty. Unemployment in the villages is one of the key factors contributing to rural poverty, and poverty drove many peasants to migrate to coastal cities, swelling the already large urban unemployment. The first issue relevant to our study is how serious is rural poverty in

---

[5]For data on employment, see SY 01, p. 108. For working-age population, see *Statistical Abstract* (SA) 01, p. 36; SY 01, p. 91. The age distribution in 1980 is assumed to be the same as that in 1982.

[6]The World Bank projects average annual GDP growth to fall from 8.4 percent in 1996–2000 to 6.9 percent in 2001–2005 (World Bank, 1997b, p. 21). Likewise, Li Jingwen anticipates GDP growth rates to drop from 9.4 percent to 8.1 percent over the same periods (Li, 1998, p. 20).

China today? Official reports and estimates by the World Bank differ sharply on this issue. According to official claims, a mere 4.8 percent of the rural population in 1998, or 42 million, were poor.[7] The World Bank estimates that 106 million rural residents lived in poverty in 1998.[8] Measures of relative poverty are lacking.[9] Nonetheless, it seems reasonable to assume that relative poverty is closely associated with the degree of income inequality. The more unequal the distribution of income, the greater the probability of a larger incidence of relative poverty. One common measure of income distribution is the Gini coefficient.[10] The World Bank estimates the rural Gini index at 40.3 percent for 1998, somewhat higher than those in other large developing Asian countries such as India and Indonesia.[11]

---

[7]Zeng, 1999, p. 632.

[8]World Bank, 2001d, p. 2. The World Bank estimate is much larger than the official estimate because the SSB uses a much more austere poverty line. The poverty line used by the World Bank is the international subsistence standard of US$ 1 per day, in 1987 purchasing power dollars. The SSB uses one that is equivalent to US$ 0.66 per day. There are reasons to believe that the SSB figures are unrealistically low. First, in calculating the poverty line, the SSB uses procurement prices to value the grain purchased or consumed by the peasants, which are below the market prices. Most poor peasants do not grow enough grain and have to purchase grain at market prices. Also, the market prices measure more realistically the alternative costs of the grain they grow and consume. According to Zhao and Griffin, 1994, p. 327, adjusting the prices would raise the official poverty line for 1988 from 260 to 291 yuan. Second, the poverty line varies with changes in the costs of living over time. Inadequate allowance for a rise in the cost of living would set the poverty line too low and understate the incidence of poverty. This is exactly the case with the SSB data. For example, the SSB reports the poverty line in 1985 and 1990 at 206 and 268 yuan, respectively, implying a 30 percent change in the rural cost of living over the period (World Bank, 1992, p. 26). Yet, the rural consumer price index rose by 65 percent over the same period (SY 01, p. 282). Third, the SSB estimates of the incidence of poverty are based on the distribution of per-capita income from its annual sample survey of rural households. The estimates are generally more conservative than those based on expenditure data (World Bank, 2001d, p. 3).

[9]People living in relative poverty are those whose incomes are below what most people regard as the minimum acceptable standard.

[10]The Gini coefficient is the ratio of the area between the diagonal and the Lorenz curve divided by the total area under the diagonal, i.e., the line of equality. The Lorenz curve shows the percentage of population (measured on the horizontal axis) that has a corresponding percentage of income (measured on the vertical scale). The coefficient ranges from 0 to 1. The larger the coefficient, the greater the inequality.

[11]World Bank, 2000c, p. 282. Note that the figures refer to indices for the economy as a whole.

What are the prospects of these problems worsening in the next decade? To address this issue, we briefly review some recent trends and their underlying factors. On the eve of economic reform, about one-third of the rural population were poor. The number dropped sharply to 12 percent by 1985 (World Bank, 1992, p. 4). The most important single factor underlying the sharp decline in poverty during this period was the rapid growth of per-capita rural income. In 1978–1985, rural per-capita income rose from 134 to 324 yuan, at an average annual growth of 13.4 percent (World Bank, 1992, p. 4). The rapid growth was the direct result of agricultural reforms during the period. The dismantling of the communes greatly enhanced the peasants' work incentives. The rise in farm procurement prices improved the terms of trade for the peasants. As the state relaxed its restrictions over labor mobility across occupations, many peasants took up nonfarm work. In particular, employment in the rural enterprises rose 2.5-fold, from 28.3 million in 1978 to 69.8 million in 1985 (SY 01, p. 111). All these factors combined to raise per-capita income and drastically reduce poverty in the rural areas.

However, during the subsequent period, 1985–1990, the incidence of poverty hardly changed (World Bank, 1992, p. 4). Apparently, by the mid-1980s, the positive effects of agricultural reform had about run their course. Further increase in per-capita income would have to come primarily from agricultural growth. Unfortunately, the average annual growth of real agricultural output per capita dropped sharply from 7.9 percent in 1980–1985 to 3.4 percent in 1985–1990 (SY 01, pp. 52, 91). By the late 1980s, there were still pockets of rural poverty in the 14 hilly provinces in interior China.[12] These provinces face more-formidable constraints to agricultural growth than the coastal plains because of their poor natural environment, underdeveloped social infrastructure, and shortage of human and financial capital.

In the 1990s, the number of rural poor began to fall again, as per-capita rural income rose at a rapid pace.[13] Several other factors also

---

[12]The 14 provinces are Inner Mongolia, Shaanxi, Shanxi, Ningxia, Qinghai, Xinjiang, Guangxi, Guizhou, Gansu, Yunnan, Sichuan, Tibet, Hebei, and Henan. The poor population in these provinces accounted for 72 percent of the total in 1989 (World Bank, 1992, p. 37).

[13]The annual growth of per-capita rural income during 1990–2000 averaged 6 percent, compared to 1 percent for 1985–1990 (SY 01, pp. 282, 323).

contributed to the rise. There had been a more rapid structural shift of the labor force into nonfarm activities where per-worker income was higher.[14] A large number of peasants from the poor areas migrated to other provinces and coastal cities looking for work, and some found employment. Rural population growth slowed in the 1990s. With the exception of Xinjiang, population growth in the 14 poor provinces all experienced a marked decline during 1990–2000, as compared to 1980–1990 (SSB, 1999; SY 01, p. 99). The period also witnessed a much greater effort by the central government to alleviate poverty.

This brief review of the developments in the last two decades suggests several key factors affecting rural poverty: the growth of per-capita agricultural output, employment opportunities in the nonfarm sector, the extent of government extraction of the peasants' net output, and the distribution of income among the peasants and across regions. One could conceive of a severe-case scenario for the next decade in which recent trends in these factors continue to be unfavorable. Agricultural growth had been slowing since the early 1980s, from 5.2 percent per year during 1980–1990 to 3.8 percent during 1990–2000 (SY 01, p. 52). Rural population growth had slowed too during the two periods, but not to the extent of agricultural growth (SY 01, p. 91). The average annual growth of nonstate, non-agricultural employment dropped from 11.2 to 6.1 percent in the two periods, respectively (SY 01, pp. 108, 110). In particular, growth of employment in the rural enterprises, which had been absorbing large numbers of rural laborers into nonfarm work, declined from 11.9 to 3.3 percent per year in 1980–1990 and 1990–2000, respectively (SY 01, p. 111).

State regulations specify that the tax burden on the peasants should be limited to no more than 5 percent of the household's per-capita net income (*China Daily*, December 23, 1991, p. 4). However, local authorities often impose many fees and levies so that the actual burden far exceeds the 5 percent ceiling.[15] Despite repeated attempts by

---

[14]Employment in the rural enterprises steadily increased. As a result of which, the share of wage income in the peasants' total incomes rose from 20 to 31 percent during 1990–2000 (SY 01, p. 323).

[15]In some cases, as much as 30–40 percent of the farmers' net incomes have been appropriated (*China Daily*, June 25, 1993, p. 4). The Ministry of Agriculture (1990, pp.

the central government to reduce the peasants' burdens, exorbitant taxes and fees remain. The basic reason is that the local cadres are under great pressure to provide social infrastructure to the local community, such as schools, family planning, road building, militia training, and health care, and they can only rely on self-raised revenues to meet budget expenditures. Given the growing needs of the local communities and a possible slowdown in agricultural growth, the share of the peasants' net income being taken by the government could remain fairly large.

Even if the incidence of absolute poverty were to remain unchanged or even decline, the severity of poverty could worsen, as was the case in the last two decades. By severity, we refer to the extent to which the poor households' incomes fall below the poverty line. Does a poor household's income fall just below, or far below the poverty line? To assess the severity of poverty, the poverty gap, which measures the additional income necessary to bring a poor person up to the poverty line, is generally used. Over time, a widening gap indicates that poverty is increasingly severe. Using this index, the World Bank has found that, in the period 1985–1998, the severity of poverty has increased (World Bank, 1992, pp. 25–26, and 2001d, pp. 2–3).

Nor have changes in the Gini index in the last two decades suggested positive results in reducing relative poverty. The World Bank finds that the rural Gini coefficient rose continually from 0.21 in 1978 to 0.31 in 1990 (World Bank, 1992, p. 23). A separate study also shows a rising trend in the 1990s (Lin, Hai, and Ping, 2000, pp. 286–300). Apparently, income distribution among individuals and across regions has become increasingly unequal. If the trend continues into the next decade, the problem of relative poverty could worsen.

If massive unemployment and rural poverty remain chronic in the next decade, what could happen to the economy? Two serious consequences are possible: One is an outburst of large-scale labor protests and peasant riots. In urban areas, migrant workers and deactivated workers are potentially major sources of social instability.

57–60) reported that in 1989, the peasants had to pay 74 types of fees or levies. In addition to levies in cash, the peasants are also obligated to contribute a certain number of labor days per year. For the present purpose, the amount of cash levies is more relevant.

Most of the migrant workers are young, with little savings and no public assistance. Desperate to survive, they could seek refuge outside the law. Deactivated workers could become disillusioned with the loss of their "iron rice bowls" and angry about meager unemployment benefits. They could direct their grievances at the government, join forces, and create a torrent of social unrest. In rural areas, the peasants' income is still relatively low, and the large labor surplus remains an unsettled, volatile force. A severe natural disaster, decisions by local governments to impose more and larger taxes, or a sharp drop in farm prices following large imports of agricultural products could threaten their survival and trigger peasant revolts. Massive demonstrations could deteriorate into sociopolitical crises if party leaders were to use the military to crush the demonstrators and their sympathizers. By then, the economy, the political leadership, and China's international relations could be thrown into chaos, as happened immediately after the Tiananmen Square incident in 1989.

Actually, a wave of labor unrest has been sweeping the nation in recent years. Incidents, sometimes involving as many as 30,000 workers, have been reported all over China, in Wuhan, Liaoyang, Daqing, Dongguan, Guiyang, Loyang, and Beijing (*The Wall Street Journal* [WSJ], January 12, 1998, p. A14, and March 14, 2002, p. A9; *Los Angeles Times*, June 10, 2002, p. A1; *Chinese Daily News* [CDN], March 25, 2002, p. A7, and April 9, 2002, p. A2). The demonstrators protested against layoffs, unpaid wages, and unfair severance packages. These protests have become more common in recent years, and their scale larger than before. However, they have not yet developed into a real crisis, partly because the protests remained localized and partly because the government has been able to contain the unrest, by targeting the handful of organizers, granting some of the workers' demands, and isolating the incidents. Likewise, many small-scale peasant riots against excessive fees and levies broke out in the 1990s.[16]

---

[16]In 1992, for example, more than 200 incidents were reported (*Far Eastern Economic Review*, July 15, 1993, pp. 68–69). In 1993, more than 170 antigovernment disturbances occurred since late 1992 (*South China Morning Post* [SCMP], June 27, 1993, p. 1). The biggest riot was the one in Renshou, Sichuan, where 10,000 peasants surrounded government buildings and attacked officials, triggered by levies to build a new road (WHP, June 13, 1993, p. 2). For specific cases of peasant unrest in seven provinces in the late 1990s, see Liu, Xu, and Liu, 1999, pp. 187–208.

Even if no large-scale riots occur, rising unemployment and rural poverty could slow economic growth through adverse effects on the key parameters of GDP growth. Take, first, their possible effects on savings. The unemployed and poor usually have little or no savings of their own. They generally have to draw on the savings of others, including the government, which takes care of most of the urban openly unemployed and the poor in remote regions. The state-owned enterprises (SOEs) and urban collective enterprises subsidize deactivated workers, workers of defunct units, and the urban disguised unemployed. Rural households bear the burden of supporting redundant farm labor. Increases in the financial support of the unemployed and the poor need not affect total savings, if they are compensated by reductions in household and government consumption expenditures. However, in the next two decades, it might be difficult for households and the government to continue such compensations for several reasons. China's population is aging rapidly.[17] Household expenditures on health care could rise rapidly because per-capita health care costs are generally higher among the aged. Moreover, the ratio of those working to the number of retirees is dropping fast.[18] That means more and more people will be living primarily on their own or others' savings. Demographic experience also shows that poor families generally have higher crude birth rates.[19] As a result, their children dependency ratio (the proportion of children age birth–14 years to those age 15–64 years) is higher than in other families.[20] An increase in the number of poor families could dissipate more savings, simply because they have more children to feed than the average family. Furthermore, household expenditures on housing could rise as a result of the government's cutting housing subsi-

---

[17]The population age 65 years or over as a share of total population is projected to increase from 6.3 percent in 2000 to 10.9 percent in 2020 (Lin and Zhai, 1996, p. 16).

[18]The ratio is expected to fall from 6:1 in 1991 to 2:1 in 2020 (Lin and Zhai, 1996, p. 349).

[19]"Crude birth rate" is a concept commonly used by demographers and economists. It refers to the average number of births during a specified period per 1,000 persons in the midperiod total population.

[20]For example, the ratios for the poor provinces Tibet, Ningxia, and Guizhou in 1999 were 57.8, 43.0, and 42.7 percent, respectively—considerably higher than the national average of 35 percent (SY 00, p. 102).

dies.[21] Of course, eliminating subsidies could increase government revenues, but the savings could be easily offset by the increase in expenditures on such urgent needs as environmental protection, reserves to liquidate the state banks' bad loans, and building a nationwide social security system. Moreover, none of this allows for the ongoing defense modernization program. The tightness of the government budget is evidenced by the persistent budget deficits and their growing size (SY 01, p. 245). If income growth should lag behind that of consumption expenditures, the savings rate would decline and the growth of capital would be adversely affected.[22]

Where possible effects of unemployment are concerned, the first point to be noted is that high unemployment could vastly increase the supply of low-cost labor. Nonetheless, unemployment and poverty could also have serious effects on the quality of labor. The major sources of human capital formation are education, training programs, and learning by doing. To be sure, China has made notable achievements in educating its people since 1978. However, increasing unemployment could disrupt the current progress in several ways. First, as noted earlier, the financial need to support increasing numbers of the poor and unemployed could strain government and household budgets. The relatively small and declining share of public educational expenditures in GDP in the last two decades suggests

---

[21]Because of the subsidies, urban households' housing expenditures accounted for only 4 percent of total consumptions in 2000, much lower than the rural households' share of 15 percent, where housing was not subsidized (SY 01, pp. 306, 326).

[22]Two caveats should be noted. First, massive unemployment results in abundant cheap labor, which could attract foreign investment. However, the lower labor cost could be offset by higher transaction costs due to a deteriorating economic environment caused by widespread poverty, urban congestion, pollution, and erosion of law and order. The assumption here is that no significant changes in these factors will occur in the next decade or so. Second, some economists argue that rural surplus labor could be used in investment in kind and thus provide a potential savings increase (Nurkse, 1953). Indeed China has been cited as a case of having successfully exploited this savings potential (Kindleberger and Herrick, 1977, p. 342; Bhaduri, 1987, p. 113). However, whether the Chinese experiment was successful is an open issue. The "Great Leap Forward" in the late 1950s, which mobilized surplus labor to build dams and backyard furnaces, was a failure. Clearly, to realize the savings potential complementary factors such as capital and technology are needed. Furthermore, an effective incentive system must be put in place to call forth additional effort from those who remain on farms, otherwise total output would fall because surplus workers have already been producing some output under the work-sharing system. In the present case, we assume that these conditions are absent.

that education has been a low-priority item for government expenditures.[23] Thus, as unemployment increases and poverty spreads, slow growth for educational expenditures is quite possible. If indeed this should happen, shortages of facilities and qualified teachers could limit the size of school enrollment. Second, at the household level, the poor and the unemployed have a hard time surviving, let alone having sufficient resources to send their children to school. An increase in unemployment and poverty could increase the number of school dropouts.[24] Third, an increasingly large number of unemployed means that the skills of more and more people will remain stagnant, because they lack opportunities to learn by doing. Fourth, the quality of labor depends not only on educational level, but also on health status. In China's poor areas, the working population suffers from poor physical health for several reasons: malnutrition, a harsh natural environment, and the lack of adequate health care. The World Bank (2001d, pp. 8–9) reports that roughly 50 percent of children in poor areas are at least mildly undernourished, few poor villages have access to safe water, and the incidence of infectious and endemic diseases is relatively high. As a result, life expectancy and the working life span of the workers are shorter than the national averages.

The effects of unemployment and poverty on the efficiency of resource use could be just as significant. We have noted that rural poverty and unemployment have driven the peasants to migrate en masse to the coastal cities. One distinct behavior of these migrants is that they usually keep the land in their villages, as a safety net against unemployment in the cities. This is understandable, because migrant workers do not have the same job security as urban workers and they are usually the first to be laid off when employers run into difficulties. Nonetheless, the scarce arable land in their home villages is be-

---

[23]The share of educational expenditures in GDP was only 2.5 percent in 1980 and dropped to 2.3 percent in 1997, discernibly lower than the world average of 3.4 and 3.3 percent for low-income countries in 1980 and 1997, respectively (World Bank, 2000c, pp. 284–285).

[24]This, in fact, has happened in the past. For example, in 1987, 46 percent of youths age 15–17 years in Guangdong were not in school, and in Hubei, 1.5 million school-age children dropped out of school, mainly because families could not afford the tuition fees (WHP, June 27, 1988, p. 10). The problem is even more serious in poverty-stricken areas. As many as half the boys and nearly all the girls in the poorest village did not attend school and would not achieve literacy (World Bank, 2001d, p. 8).

ing underutilized. The practice also prevents the consolidation of land into larger and more-efficient farms.

Another possible effect of rural poverty on land use is that more-intensive use of arable land in poor regions could result in lower soil fertility. In the poor's struggle to survive, environmental consequences are of secondary importance. Heavy dependence on crops, particularly grain, puts increasing pressure on their poor-quality land. Population growth forces them to reclaim more and more inferior land. Overexploitation, soil erosion, and deforestation inevitably follow. The government thus faces a dilemma. If nothing is done to protect the environment, a vicious circle could ensue. Poverty leads to environmental deterioration, and a poor environment lowers productivity and depresses the peasants' income. If, however, the government decides to reverse the trend, substantial resources would be required to improve the environment, and quite possibly, resources would have to be diverted from other uses, possibly from more productive ones.

By definition, unemployment entails idle labor, and an increase in unemployment means wastage of more labor resources. In China's case, there are two other possible sources of inefficiency. The first is that massive unemployment could lead to local protectionism. As the World Bank notes (2001d, p. 26),

> rising urban unemployment has resulted in a growing intolerance for rural migration by urban governments and populations. So as to protect urban workers, urban governments have in some cases tried to segment the labor market by requiring urban employers to hire migrants only for unskilled, menial jobs.

An increase in unemployment in the next decade could further intensify the rise of local protectionism.

Second, in rural areas, the rural unemployed who migrate are generally young and better educated (Yang, 1997, p. 61). The exodus of educated youths thus drains the limited human capital from the villages and could adversely affect productivity on the farms.[25] Meanwhile, these better-educated youth are either unemployed or, in

---

[25]Such negative effects have been found in Sichuan (WHP, June 9, 1988, p. 10).

many cases, hired to do unskilled work in the cities. An increase in internal migration of the rural poor and unemployed thus could result in a misallocation of the educated few.[26]

Unemployment could adversely affect capital use as well. Under the work-sharing system, redundant workers generally require some capital investments, such as floor space, tools, and equipment. In an important sense, capital goods to accommodate redundant workers are also redundant. Any increase in the disguised unemployed could result in more wastage of resources. Furthermore, as noted earlier, unemployment could increase transaction costs for business activities, because of its unfavorable effects on law and order, the environment, and labor disputes. Indeed, crime rates in the coastal cities climbed sharply since the influx of migrant workers.[27] Incidents of social unrest not only disrupt normal economic activities, they also induce the society to divert resources to less productive uses, such as to measures for controlling crime and protecting private property.

In the past, the government has stepped in to help the poor and unemployed. However, the allocation of resources by the government has not always been based on economic considerations. For example, the allocation of relief funds was politically biased. Counties with favorable political credentials and strong supporters—such as old revolutionary bases—were provided poverty relief despite having per-capita income levels twice the poverty line (World Bank, 2001d, p. 6). This means that counties in greater need of relief were deprived

---

[26]It should be noted that the effects of internal migration on resource allocations are not all unfavorable. Some of the migrants acquire formal education by going to adult schools. Others go through technical training conducted by their employers. Still others learn new skills, acquire management techniques, and develop a network of personal and business connections. Their subsequent return to their home villages could enhance capital formation in the remote areas. However, such benefits should not be overstated. Most migrant workers are hired to do the "low level" jobs that provide little opportunity for skill formation, and few of the migrant workers who return become entrepreneurs.

[27]See *Asian Wall Street Journal* (AWSJ), February 3–4, 1995, pp. 1, 8. In 1984, there were only 0.5 million criminal cases. It rose to 1.6 million in 1996, as the registered urban unemployed increased from 2.4 to 10.9 million over the same period (CAS, 1998, pp. 163–164). According to another estimate, 56 percent of the criminal cases in Shanghai, Beijing, and Tianjin during July 1993 to June 1994 were committed by the unemployed (Yang, 1997, p. 12). Elsewhere, clashes between the police and the unemployed have been reported (SCMP, December 6, 1995, p. 1; CDN, October 16, 2001, p. A16).

of support. Furthermore, the more-permissive policies regarding population control among minorities tend to perpetuate their low per-capita income status. If such perverse policies should continue, more resource waste could result.

For a rough estimate of the potential economic losses resulting from these circumstances, we use a simple growth accounting framework to project GDP growth: first, in a sustained growth scenario where economic progress continues without major disruptions; and second, under worsening conditions of unemployment and rural poverty. We take the World Bank's projection of GDP growth at 6.6 percent per year as a benchmark estimate of sustained economic growth for the next decade.[28] The World Bank projection is based on the following assumptions: (1) the investment rate remains at 35 percent (World Bank, 1997b, p. 20); a capital-output ratio of 3 is implicitly assumed so that physical capital grows at 11.5 percent per year;[29] (2) labor grows at 0.8 percent per year (World Bank, 1997c, p. 34); (3) the growth of human capital is 1 percent per year;[30] (4) the output elasticities of physical capital, human capital, and labor are assumed to be 0.4, 0.3, and 0.3, respectively (World Bank, 1997b, p. 106); and (5) the growth of total factor productivity is projected at 1.5 percent per year (World Bank, 1997b, p. 21).

We postulate two adverse scenarios in which the savings rate drops by 1 and 3 percent of GDP, as a result of mounting subsidies to the

---

[28]See World Bank, 1997b, pp. 20–21. The projections are originally for 1995–2020. We assume it to be the same as that for 2000–2010.

[29]The implicit capital-output ratio is reconstructed from the World Bank data as follows. The contribution of capital to GDP growth, 4.6 percentage points, is first obtained by subtracting those of labor (0.5 percentage points) and total factor productivity (1.5 percentage points) from GDP growth (6.6 percent). The contribution of labor is derived by multiplying its annual growth (0.8 percent) by its output elasticity (0.6). Similarly, the growth of capital (11.5 percent) is obtained by dividing its contribution (4.6 percent) by its output elasticity (0.4). The implied capital-output ratio is derived by dividing the investment rate (35 percent) by capital growth (11.5 percent). For sources of data, see text.

[30]The contribution of human capital growth to GDP growth (0.3 percentage points) is derived as a residual from GDP growth (6.6 percent), physical capital contribution (4.6 percent), labor growth contribution (0.2 percent, which is the product of labor growth [0.8 percent] and the output elasticity of labor [0.3]), and total factor productivity growth (1.5 percent). Given the output elasticity of human capital (0.3), the implied growth of human capital is 1 percent per year.

unemployed and poor and of increases in public and private expenditures to maintain law and order, which have never been firmly established in the first place. Furthermore, we assume that the annual growth of labor falls from 0.8 percent in the benchmark model to 0.7 and 0.5 percent, that the growth of human capital, from 1.0 to 0.8 and 0.6 percent, and that total factor productivity growth drops from 1.5 to 1.4 and 1.3 percent, as the decline in the investment rate also lowers the demand for labor, as less expenditures on education and less opportunities to acquire formal or informal training slow the accumulation of human capital, and as more uneven distribution of income across regions and individual groups generates social discontent and rising local protectionism. Under these assumptions for the two adverse scenarios, GDP growth falls to 6.3 and 5.8 percent, the loss being 0.3 and 0.8 percentage points, respectively.

Chapter Three

ECONOMIC EFFECTS OF CORRUPTION

"Corruption" is difficult to define in a way that facilitates measurement, but it can be viewed as private payments, whether pecuniary or in-kind, undermining either efficient or inefficient rules or substituting for the absence of such rules. Obvious examples are bribes for needed permits and the like; the range of potential forms that corruption might take is limited only by the human imagination. It may be the case that certain institutions—democratic choice of public officials, a free press, an independent judiciary itself somehow constrained by a rule of law, thus presenting a certain chicken-and-egg problem—reduce the potential opportunities for corrupt behavior, but that is a large issue beyond the scope of this project.

Instead, we ask a far narrower question: What is the likely economic effect for China, as a crude quantitative exercise, of a substantial increase in corruption as an economic quasi-institution? We assume for analytic purposes that the effect is negative, although even that is not entirely obvious; as noted above, corruption can undermine both good law and bad. But for a China with economic institutions evolving away from those characterizing state socialism, and with a growing economy and middle and upper classes interested in rules upon which they can rely and in a reduction in the prospective degree to which their (economic) interests can be threatened by extralegal behavior, it is reasonable to assume that corruption is a threat to the evolution of an enforced rule of law and thus would impose net economic costs.

Two surveys of parameters that crudely serve as proxies for "corruption" were reviewed. The first is the *Economic Freedom of the*

World 2002 Annual Report, a "survey of surveys" by James Gwartney et al. and published by the Fraser Institute (Vancouver, B.C.) in 2003.[1] Among the five classes of parameters yielding the economic freedom index, "Legal Structure and Security of Property Rights" and "Regulation of Credit, Labor, and Business" contain variables that in our judgment would enjoy broad agreement as components of a usable "corruption" index. The former comprises judicial independence, impartial courts, protection of intellectual property, military interference, and integrity of the legal system. The latter comprises administrative obstacles for new business, time spent with government bureaucracy, ease of starting a new business, and irregular payments to government officials. The indices are presented on a scale of 1 to 10, with 10 being the "most free." Table 3.1 presents these data for China, derived from surveys used in Gwartney et al., 2002.

For comparison purposes, Table 3.2 presents similar data for 2000 for India, Indonesia, Russia, Turkey, and the United States.

What is interesting in the China case from Table 3.1 is that the indices underlying "legal structure and security of property rights" uniformly have declined (worsened) since 1985, while those underlying "regulation of business" have improved since 1995, although only two observations are available. Cross-sectional comparisons are

Table 3.1

"Corruption" Parameters for China

Parameter	1980	1985	1990	1995	2000
Legal structure and security of property rights	n.a.	6.8	5.8	5.0	4.1
Regulation of business	n.a.	n.a.	n.a.	4.4	5.6
Economic freedom summary rating	3.7	4.9	4.6	5.1	5.3

SOURCE: Gwartney et al., 2002.

NOTES: Ratings are on a scale of 1 to 10, with 10 being the "most free." n.a. = not available.

---

[1]The ranking data are derived from the *Global Competitiveness Report* and from the *International Country Risk Guide.* The Fraser Institute is an independent economic and social research and educational organization.

Table 3.2

Comparative Indices for Several Nations for 2000

Nation	Legal Structure/Security of Property Rights	Business Regulation
China	4.1	5.6
India	6.0	5.9
Indonesia	3.4	4.8
Russia	4.4	5.1
Turkey	5.4	5.9
United States	9.2	8.3

SOURCE: Gwartney et al., 2002.

problematic for these subcomponents of the overall index for economic freedom because of differences in data availability over time. However, the indices place China roughly in the middle quintile among nations, and the five quintiles for the summary economic freedom index have average annual percentage economic growth rates that differ sharply; from the lowest to the highest, they are, respectively, –0.85, 1.13, 1.44, 1.57, and 2.56.

For purposes of our "adversities" analysis, let us assume that corruption in China worsens so that the future relevant indices fall to levels represented in the lowest of the quintiles. Such deterioration might occur for many reasons and through many channels. For example, government contracts might increasingly be directed toward less-efficient, higher-cost SOEs, or formally "privatized" SOEs in which government entities hold controlling shares; or preferences might be accorded to those private firms whose lenders join the Chinese Communist Party (CCP), and/or are willing to share their profits with the CCP.

The economic freedom summary rating is the composite rating for each of the nations in the survey; it is that summary rating (by quintile) that is correlated with economic growth in the Gwartney et al., 2002, study. Like the "corruption" parameters discussed above, this summary rating places China roughly in the middle quintile among the nations, although the summary rating for China has been improving more-or-less steadily since 1980. Note also that the summary economic freedom index comprises five classes of parameters; "Legal Structure and Security of Property Rights" is one of the five, while "Regulation of Business" is one component (among three) of another

("Regulation of Credit, Labor, and Business"). Under the crude assumption that each of the parameter classes contributes equally to the summary rating[2] and, in turn, to differences in economic growth rates, "corruption" would account for somewhat more than one-fifth of the observed differences in economic growth rates ("Legal Structure and Security of Property Rights" is one of the five economic freedom components and "Regulation of Business" is one-third of another component). Since that difference between the ratings in the third and last quintiles is about two percentage points of growth, a crude estimate is that Chinese economic growth would decline by about 0.5 percent per year were Chinese corruption to worsen so that its index fell into the lowest quintile. This may be an underestimate in that a sharp worsening of corruption would not occur in a vacuum; it would be more likely to be a coincident or ancillary effect of other adverse trends harming Chinese growth, a point to which we return below.

The second survey of interest is the "Corruption Perceptions Index" published by Transparency International.[3] This index is a summary of polls reflecting the views of country analysts, academics, and businessmen. Table 3.3 presents the index data for China for 1995 through 2001.

Table 3.4 contrasts the Gwartney et al., 2002, and Transparency International, 2001, ratings. Both the Gwartney et al., 2002, "Regulation" rating and the Transparency International, 2001, "Corruption Perceptions" rating show moderate improvement since the mid-1990s. The former ranks China in the middle quintile, while the latter ranks China in the fourth. The Gwartney et al., 2002, "Legal Structure" rating shows a steady decline since the mid-1980s; this may suggest that "corruption" stems more from required dealings with

---

[2]In fact, in the Gwartney et al., 2002, methodology, the summary rating is the average of the five parameter classes.

[3]See Transparency International, *Global Corruption Report 2001*, Berlin, Germany, 2001, at www.transparency.org. Transparency International is an international non-governmental organization devoted to combating corruption. The data underlying the index are reported by the World Economic Forum, the Institute for Management Development, PricewaterhouseCoopers, the World Bank, the Economist Intelligence Unit, Freedom House, and the Political and Economic Risk Consultancy (Hong Kong).

Table 3.3

Corruption Perceptions Index for China

Year	Index	Rank Among Nations
1995	2.2	40 of 41
1996	2.4	45 of 47
1997	2.9	41 of 52
1998	3.5	52 of 85
1999	3.4	58 of 99
2000	3.1	63 of 90

SOURCE: Transparency International, 2001.
NOTE: Ratings are on a scale of 1 to 10. A higher index value indicates less corruption.

Table 3.4

Ratings Comparisons

Year	Legal Structure	Regulation	Corruption Perceptions
1985	6.8	n.a.	n.a.
1990	5.8	n.a.	n.a.
1995	5.0	4.4	2.2
1996	n.a.	n.a.	2.4
1997	n.a.	n.a.	2.9
1998	n.a.	n.a.	3.5
1999	n.a.	n.a.	3.4
2000	4.1	5.6	3.1
2001	n.a.	n.a.	3.5

SOURCES: Tables 3.1 and 3.3 above.
NOTE: n.a. = not available.

government officials than from the nature of formal legal institutions per se, which may affect economic growth directly and corrupt practices only indirectly. In any event, there is no obvious inconsistency between the Gwartney et al., 2002, and Transparency International, 2001, findings for China; however, the latter does not correlate the Corruption Perceptions Index with economic growth.

Again, a dramatic increase in corrupt practices in China, as noted above, would be likely to reflect some deeper set of trends increasing private incentives to engage in corrupt behavior. An example might be a large increase in explicit taxation in the face of severe budget deficits, increasing incentives to operate businesses off the books, with side payments to various public officials. Such hidden economic activity might entail higher costs of various kinds—for example, the higher taxation/side payment system might induce a substitution of labor for capital so as partially to avoid large fixed investments that could be taxed away, whether formally or by corrupt officials—so that corruption in this case would be correlated with lower economic output, although one could argue that it is the higher taxation that is the real source of the reduced economic product. More fundamentally, sectors with greater susceptibility to demands for extralegal payments will tend to decline relative to other sectors, other things equal, yielding less aggregate output for a given supply of inputs and available technology. Another example might be the use of inflation as an implicit tax instrument with which to acquire real resources for the public sector, combined with price controls intended to mask the inflationary pressures. Such price controls can be predicted to yield shortages, with a subsequent requirement for some nonprice mechanism with which to allocate resources and intermediate and final goods. It is not difficult to envision the widespread growth of bribery—corruption—as a substitute allocation tool. Again, we would expect economic growth to fall, primarily as a result of the inflation tax and the economic inefficiencies caused by the controls.

And so our crude estimate of 0.5 percent in terms of reduced GDP growth in the case of a sharp increase in Chinese corruption does not seem unreasonable; certainly, there appears to be no reason to believe it is unrealistically high. The adverse GDP effects of corruption, however, are likely to be correlated with the conceptually separate consequences yielded by other parameters and policies (e.g., tax policies, protection of property rights, etc.), which are likely to reduce growth directly and also indirectly by engendering an increase in the extent to which corrupt practices are observed. Separation of the marginal effects of corruption per se would not be a trivial exercise.

Note that the economic cost of corruption is not, crudely, the amount of money that changes hands. In pure economic terms, that is a wealth transfer that for the economy as a whole is neither a cost nor a benefit. Instead, the economic cost of corruption is the reduced economic output that results from it, as individuals and businesses make adjustments in the face of corruption among public officials and its attendant effects in reducing the efficiency of resource use, hence, reducing the aggregate size of the output basket that can be produced from the resources available. Such inefficiency might take the form of resource use in less productive activities, resource use by less productive individuals and businesses, and the like.

It was noted above that a sharp increase in corruption, however defined or measured, would be likely to result from changes in other parameters or conditions yielding an increase in the incentives for corrupt behavior. At the same time, it is wholly plausible that corrupt practices might grow or decline even in the absence of an important shift in underlying parameters. Certainly it is unclear whether current conditions in China of uneven economic reform and (perhaps slowing) economic growth are likely to yield an increase, decrease, or no major change in corruption. On the one hand, the ongoing visible anticorruption efforts of the government might yield such a decline, although those efforts are not inconsistent with an increase in the same way that, say, police forces might exert greater efforts against burglary precisely because it is increasing. On the other hand, a growing economy generally might offer greater opportunities for corrupt behavior, in the same sense that a growing economy offers expanding opportunities for the use of straightforward tax instruments, and an expanding public-sector investment program in particular might be accompanied by an increase in corrupt practices in the context of contract awards and the like.

Professor Angang Hu offers an estimate of the economic cost of Chinese corruption for 1995–1998 of 13.2–16.8 percent of GDP.[4] Note that Hu attempts to measure the level of corruption, while we are focused upon the GDP effects of a large increase in corruption. Accordingly, our respective findings are not necessarily inconsistent. Hu includes several categories within the classification "corruption." As discussed below, his calculations include both real inefficiency costs (or "deadweight losses") and wealth transfers from the broad economy to those favored. His calculations thus are important but may suffer from an upward bias.

- *Dual price systems presumably protected by government officials.* Hu notes that this practice yields high prices for important in-

[4]Angang Hu, "Corruption: The Largest Social Pollution in China," unpublished manuscript; and Angang Hu, "China: Corruption and Anti-Corruption Strategies," unpublished briefing, Tsinhua University, Beijing.

puts in some sectors; this is very likely to yield inefficiency, that is, a reduction in aggregate output, but the high prices (or the high profits earned by those favored) themselves are not an economic "cost." Nor are any corrupt payments to officials in pursuit of high administered prices, strictly speaking, an economic cost of corruption; although, again, Hu is correct in that the high prices yield real costs in the form of GDP lower than otherwise would be the case.[5]

- *Awards of economic monopolies.* Again, the monopolistic pricing likely to result creates inefficiency in the form of resource misallocation and in the form of investments in efforts to obtain monopolies or to avoid the effects of monopolies; but the high prices and profits themselves are not a corruption "cost."

- *Dual systems for various kinds of governmental favoritism, whether for trading rights or other favors.* Again, neither the payments to corrupt officials nor the high profits that result, strictly speaking, are economic costs, but the resulting resource misallocation is.

- *Underground economic activities engendered or facilitated by corrupt practices.* An example of such activity might be the drug trade. The economic cost—again—is the decline in the value of aggregate output, rather than, say, total spending on such underground activities.[6]

- *Tax evasion facilitated by corrupt practices.* The economic cost of such evasion is not the sum of tax payments avoided. Instead, it is the resulting reduction in the size of the public sector under the assumption that the tax evasion yields too little government spending; alternatively, it might be the additional economic costs created by the substitution of tax instruments less efficient than those being evaded.

---

[5]At the same time, real resources consumed in efforts to influence public officials corruptly are a real cost of corruption; a trivial example might be construction of a palatial home as a bribe, to the extent that the home proves more costly than what the recipient official would have obtained otherwise.

[6]Note that the "value" of output is a highly normative concept. As a crude generalization, market economies value output baskets at market prices as determined in markets driven by individual preferences. Other value systems might yield sharply different valuations; the labor theory of value is an old (and tired) example.

- *Distortion of government investment and expenditures.* The cost of such an outcome is not, say, the reduction (or expansion) in government spending. It is instead the decline in the value of aggregate output including government output.

As noted above, one problem with the Hu estimate is the blending of real economic costs with pure wealth exchanges, reduced tax payments, and the like; but at the same time, some substantial inefficiency costs are likely to be captured by his estimates. Derivation of an estimate of the economic cost of a sharp increase in corruption less crude than that discussed above (0.5 percent of GDP) lies beyond the scope of this book. Note that the Hu estimate, whatever its problems, is given for the cost of corruption as a steady state exercise, rather than as an estimate of the cost of a sharp increase in corruption, the more relevant parameter in the context of an "adversities" inquiry. It does seem, however, that Hu's "steady state" estimate of 13.2–16.8 percent of GDP is unreasonably higher than our "adversities" estimate of 0.5 percent of GDP; one might surmise, after all, that a sharp increase in corruption would yield a cost increase greater than one-thirtieth of that already prevailing. Our conjecture is that Hu's blending of true economic costs with wealth transfers is a large source of this problem. At the same time, perhaps our "adversities" estimate is too low; if so, it is "conservative" in the appropriate direction for purposes of this analysis.

.

PART II

SECTORAL FAULT LINES

Chapter Four

EPIDEMIC DISEASE: A WILD CARD IN CHINA'S ECONOMIC FUTURE?

Is communicable disease a factor that might seriously impede China's economic ascent over the next decade or two? Could the outbreak and unchecked spread of epidemic illness—in particular, HIV/AIDS—in the years immediately ahead prove so devastating in and of itself as to alter China's expected development trajectory?

These are questions that demand highly speculative responses—and such responses are intrinsically problematic. Conjectures about momentous but as yet entirely hypothetical future contingencies can be unsatisfying and unconvincing, precisely to the degree that they lack rigor and empirical support. These sorts of contingencies are therefore perhaps best explored through what might be termed "rigorous speculation."

Rigorous speculation about prospective adverse economic consequences for China from lethal infectious contagion would require us to focus upon a number of topics. First, we must outline China's performance in improving local health levels over the past half century and how that performance has affected infectious and parasitic disease. Second, we must attempt to describe China's current health profile (and the role of communicable illness within the overall profile) and to place that profile in international perspective. Third, we must attempt to describe plausibly the reasons (if any) that an upsurge of infectious disease could be expected in modern-day China. Fourth, we must try to model plausible trajectories for any such epidemic outbreaks. Finally, we must attempt to think through the sorts of costs—and attempt to describe the probable magnitudes of those same costs—that would be visited upon China by the hypothesized upsurge in epidemic disease. This chapter will briefly address each of the aforementioned topics.

CHINA'S HEALTH PROGRESS SINCE THE "LIBERATION": A LONG MARCH AGAINST INFECTIOUS AND PARASITIC DISEASE

To this very day, China's demographic data are distinctly limited: Birth and death registration are nearly complete only in some major urban areas, and the quality of other demographic data (such as census returns and national surveys) is still a matter of discussion among foreign specialists.[1] Such data questions notwithstanding, there is no doubt that China has dramatically transformed health conditions and mortality risks since the Chinese Communist Party's official Liberation of the Mainland on October 1, 1949. Figure 4.1 illustrates China's changing health situation, using the summary index of estimated life expectation at birth. In the early 1950s, according to reconstructions by demographer Sheng Luo, life expectancy in China was under 45 years; by the year 2000, according to projections by the World Bank, it was about 70 years.[2] By those figures, life expectancy in China jumped by over a quarter century in less than two generations. Reconstructions by the United Nations Population Division imply an even greater improvement in life expectancy: an increase of about 29 years over the course of four and a half decades, from about 41 in 1950–1955 to about 70 in 1995–2000.[3] If we were to use the Liberation as the starting point, China's long-term performance might look even more striking: According to internal but not im-

---

[1]For contrasting assessments, see Jean-Clause Chesnais and Laurent Murawiec, "China's Statistics: A Hologram of Errors," Paris: Institute National d'Etudes Demographiques, unpublished paper; and William Lavely, "First Impressions of the 2000 Census of China," *Population and Development Review*, Vol. 27, No. 4, December 2001, pp. 755–770.

[2]World Bank, *World Development Indicators 2001* (CD-ROM), 2001a.

[3]United Nations Population Division, *World Population Prospects: The 2000 Revisions* (CD-ROM), New York, 2000.

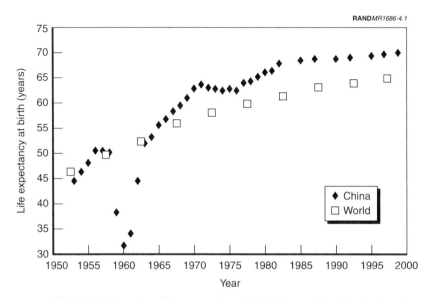

SOURCE: Sheng Luo, "Reconstruction of Life Tables and Age Distributions for the Population of China, by Year, from 1953 to 1982," New York: United Nations, World Population Prospects, 2000 revision.

Figure 4.1—Life Expectancy Circa 1950–2000: China Versus the World

plausible official calculations, China's life expectancy at birth in 1949 was only 35 years—suggesting as much as a 36-year surge between 1949 and 2000.[4]

The road to low mortality in China, we should note, was not an uninterrupted one: rather, after the "Great Leap Forward" campaign of 1957–1958, China plunged headlong into catastrophic famine, as reflected by the collapse of life expectancy in the 1959–1962 period in Figure 4.1.[5] Yet if we compare circumstances in the early 1950s with those in the late 1990s, we can see that China's long-term improve-

---

[4]*Xinhua,* December 12, 2000; reprinted as "Infectious Diseases Drops [sic] in Past 50 Years, Raising Life Span by 36 Years in PRC," in U.S. Foreign Broadcast Information Service (hereafter, FBIS), FBIS-CHI-2000-1212, December 12, 2000.

[5]For an account of that disaster, consult Jasper Becker, *Hungry Ghosts: Mao's Secret Famine,* New York: Free Press, 1997.

ments in life expectancy were greater than those for the rest of the world taken as a whole. In other words, in the early 1950s, expectation of life at birth in China was below the world average, whereas it was about four or five years above the world's average by the late 1990s.

Communist China's progress in improving the survival schedules for its general population can be viewed in large measure as the consequence of a successful long-term process of controlling infectious disease. Although China itself lacked comprehensive and reliable cause-of-death statistics in the 1950s (as it does today), a strong and international correspondence between overall mortality levels and cause-of-death structures has been established through data from other countries (both Western and non-Western).[6] According to those modeled patterns, a reduction of age-standardized death rates from about 25 per 1,000 to about 10 per 1,000—roughly speaking, China's accomplishment between the early 1950s and the late 1990s—would be attributed overwhelmingly to the decline in deaths from infectious and parasitic disease: influenza, tuberculosis, and cholera, among many others.[7]

Thus, the very fact that China has gone from being a high-mortality country to a low-mortality country can be taken in and of itself as powerful evidence that China has effectively checked and suppressed epidemic disease. Beijing's own rendition of that record may not be far from the mark:

> Before 1949, people were severely affected by epidemics and varieties of endemics due to lack of medical care. Diseases such as cholera, smallpox, diphtheria, typhoid and malaria plagued the country and threatened many lives in the first half of the century. . . . In the past 50 years, the nation has made great achieve-

---

[6]Samuel H. Preston and Verne E. Nelson, "Structure and Change in Causes of Death: An International Survey," *Population Studies*, Vol. XXVIII, No. 1, March 1974, pp. 19–51.

[7]Preston and Nelson's work suggests that reduced mortality from infectious disease would be predicted to account for over two-thirds of an overall decline in the standardized death rate, from 25 per 1,000 to 10 per 1,000. Most of the remainder, according to their model, would be attributed to reduced deaths from "other and unknown" causes—and some important part of that remainder might also be related to undiagnosed infectious disease.

> ments in building up its Medicare system. . . . Infectious diseases like smallpox and measles have been wiped out in China and chincough, diphtheria and poliomyelitis are under control.[8]

Although much of Communist China's progress against infectious and communicable disease may have been registered in the Maoist era,[9] morbidity and mortality due to such diseases have continued to decline after the historic December 1978 turn in official economic strategy.

With respect to mortality, for example, Judith Banister has noted that age-specific death rates for Chinese children in the age 1–4 cohort fell by half between 1981 and 1995; she attributes this drop to both "a national campaign to immunize a very high proportion of children against the major diseases of childhood" and "improvements in rural water supplies [which reduced the risk of child death from] dysentery, diarrhea, typhoid, cholera and intestinal parasites."[10]

Other indicators of epidemic and communicable disease have signaled continuing, and sometimes major, improvement in the Deng and post-Deng era. Between 1983 and 1997, for example, the annual number of cases of malaria reported to the World Health Organization (WHO) fell in China by about 90 percent, from about 265,000 to about 27,000.[11]

CHINA'S CURRENT HEALTH PROFILE IN INTERNATIONAL AND GEOGRAPHIC PERSPECTIVE

To appreciate the risk that infectious and parasitic diseases (including epidemic diseases) currently pose to public health in China, we can take two separate but related approaches. First, we

---

[8]*Xinhua,* December 10, 2000; *Xinhua,* December 12, 2000 (reprinted as "Infectious Diseases Drop in Past 50 Years, Raising Life Span by 36 Years in PRC," FBIS-CHI-2000-1212, December 12, 2000).

[9]See Judith Banister, *China's Changing Population,* Stanford, Calif.: Stanford University Press, 1987, especially Chapters 3 and 4.

[10]Judith Banister, "Population, Public Health and the Environment in China," *China Quarterly,* December 1998, pp. 986–1015.

[11]"Malaria, 1982–1997," *Weekly Epidemiological Review,* Vol. 74, No. 32, 1999, pp. 265–270.

can cast the issue in international perspective; thereafter, we can examine the issue in Chinese domestic, geographical perspective.

An international perspective can be gleaned from some of the work of the WHO. Since the early 1990s, as part of a major effort to quantify the "global burden of disease," WHO researchers have been striving to estimate both detailed cause of death patterns for major regions of the world and also "disability adjusted life years" (DALYs)—a new composite measure reflecting the effects of mortality plus illness plus injury—for worldwide populations.[12]

That research project is controversial, and its findings are not universally accepted by specialists.[13] Considerable surmise was required to present comprehensive estimates of cause of death for regions where mortality registration is far from complete; moreover, any metric weighting the "burden of disease" necessarily relies upon both important and inescapably arbitrary assumptions. Whatever their shortcomings, the WHO "global burden of disease" numbers are nevertheless illustrative—and thus informative for our purposes.

Table 4.1 depicts the WHO's estimate of the proportion of overall deaths in 1998 due to specific diseases in China and three other regions of the world. The first comparator is India—Asia's other demographic giant and arguably a rising economic and geopolitical power in its own right. The second grouping is the High-Income WHO Member States: the roughly 900 million persons living in North America, Western Europe, Japan, Australia, New Zealand, and a few other, smaller societies.[14] The final grouping is the collectivity of Low- and Middle-Income WHO Europe member states: This group-

---

[12]See, World Bank, *World Development Report 1993*, New York: Oxford University Press, 1993; and Christopher J. L. Murray and Alan D. Lopez, eds., *Global Burden of Disease: A Comprehensive Assessment of Mortality and Disability for Diseases, Injuries and Risk Factors in 1990 and Projected to 2020*, Cambridge, Mass.: Harvard University Press, 1996.

[13]For critiques of the approach and the work, see Kenneth C. James and Susan D. Foster, "Weighing Up Disability," *Lancet*, Vol. 354, July 10, 1999, pp. 87–88; and Sudhir Anand and Kara Hanson, "Disability-Adjusted Life Years: A Critical Review," *Journal of Health Economics*, Vol. 16, No. 6, December 1997, pp. 685–702.

[14]Israel, Hong Kong, Singapore, a few small Middle East oil-exporting states, and a handful of small, island societies from the Caribbean, the Mediterranean, the Indian Ocean, and the Pacific.

ing essentially demarcates the post-communist states of Europe (i.e., the former Soviet Bloc, the former Yugoslavia, Albania),[15] with the Russian Federation itself accounting for over a third of the collectivity's total population.

A number of interesting differences between China and these three other major population groupings are suggested by Table 4.1 (among them, that injuries and respiratory diseases may figure much more prominently in China's own particular patterns of death). But our focus in this chapter is on the risk of death from infectious and parasitic ("communicable") illness.

According to the WHO estimates, communicable conditions accounted for about 5 percent of China's fatalities in 1998. What does that proportion signify? On the one hand, it would be distinctly greater than the negligible 1.5 percent of high-income country deaths attributed to infectious and parasitic disease. On the other, it would be vastly less than the roughly 23 percent of India's mortality attributed to communicable conditions. From the standpoint of mortality structure, the role of infectious and parasitic illnesses in China's overall death patterns looks closest to that of the former Soviet Bloc, although communicable disease would appear to account for a slightly higher share of overall mortality in the former than the latter (5 percent versus 3.5 percent).

If the WHO figures are to be trusted, as of 1998 China's primary infectious cause of death was tuberculosis, accounting for just under 3 percent of total mortality; China's five leading infectious/parasitic causes of death accounted for 4.4 percent of total deaths. In India, by contrast, the top five communicable diseases accounted for about 19 percent of overall mortality—about four times the share in China; in

---

[15]Two former communist regions are counted within High-Income Europe: the former German Democratic Republic (now the "new Federal States" in the Federal Republic of Germany) and Slovenia from the former Yugoslavia. Further, one never-communist country is included in WHO's Low- and Middle-Income Europe taxonomy: Turkey. Turkey, though, accounts for less than a seventh of the total population of that grouping. Low- and Middle-Income Europe therefore is, for most intents and purposes, a proxy for post-communist Europe.

Table 4.1

Mortality Structure by Cause of Death: China and Selected Regions, 1998
(percentage of total deaths by cause)

Disease	China	India	High-Income WHO Member States	Low- and Middle-Income Europe
Communicable diseases, maternal, perinatal, and nutritional	11.3	42.8	6.3	9.4
(of which, infectious and parasitic diseases)	4.9	22.7	1.5	3.5
Tuberculosis	2.8	4.5	0.2	1.0
STDs excluding HIV	0.0	0.6	0.0	0.0
HIV/AIDS	0.1	1.9	0.4	0.1
Diarrheal diseases	0.7	7.6	0.1	1.1
Childhood diseases	0.3	4.6	0.1	0.6
Meningitis	0.3	0.4	0.1	0.2
Hepatitis	0.3	0.2	0.1	0.1
Malaria	0.0	0.2	0.0	0.0
Tropical diseases	0.0	0.3	0.0	0.0
Leprosy	0.0	0.0	0.0	0.0
Dengue	0.0	0.1	0.0	0.0
Japanese encephalitis	0.0	0.0	0.0	0.0
Trachoma	0.0	0.0	0.0	0.0
Intestinal nematode infections	0.1	0.0	0.0	0.0
Other infectious diseases	0.3	2.2	0.6	0.4
Maternal conditions, perinatal conditions, nutritional deficiencies	2.9	9.0	1.0	2.5
Noncommunicable conditions	76.5	47.9	87.4	80.8
Malignant neoplasms	19.8	7.0	25.1	14.7

Table 4.1—continued

Disease	China	India	High-Income WHO Member States	Low- and Middle-Income Europe
Cardiovascular diseases	31.7	30.2	44.7	54.1
Ischaemic heart disease	9.5	15.8	23.5	26.9
Cerebrovascular disease	15.8	6.0	11.1	15.5
Other cardiac diseases	6.5	8.5	10.2	11.7
Neuropsychiatric disorders	1.0	1.1	2.8	1.6
Respiratory diseases	15.9	3.0	4.9	4.2
Other noncommunicable diseases	8.1	6.5	9.9	6.2
Injuries	12.2	9.9	6.2	9.8
Unintentional	7.1	7.7	4.1	5.6
Road traffic accidents	1.9	2.3	1.8	2.0
Poisoning	0.7	0.3	0.2	0.9
Falls	0.8	0.5	1.0	0.6
Fires	0.3	1.4	0.1	0.2
Drowning	1.5	1.0	0.2	0.5
Other unintentional injuries	2.0	2.1	0.9	1.3
Intentional	5.1	2.1	2.1	4.2
Self-inflicted	4.4	1.3	1.6	1.9
Homicide and violence	0.6	0.8	0.5	0.9
War	0.0	0.0	0.0	1.4

SOURCE: World Health Organization, *The World Health Report 1999*, Geneva, Annex Table 2.

post-communist Europe, the corresponding share was 3 percent, as against under 1 percent for the high-income countries.

The WHO's DALY is intended to reckon to aggregate mortality, illness, and disability into an internationally comparable index. The WHO's estimates of per-capita DALYs in 1998 for China and the three other groupings under consideration are shown in Figure 4.2.

China's overall health profile, according to these numbers, is much better than India's—and differences in the burden of illness due to infectious and parasitic diseases are said to account for most of that discrepancy. Interestingly, WHO numbers suggest that China's overall burden of disease is somewhat lower than that of post-communist Europe, although the proportion of the overall burden

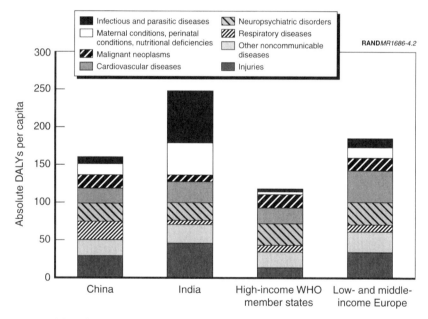

SOURCE: World Health Organization, *The World Health Report 1999*, Geneva, Annex Table 2.

Figure 4.2—WHO-Estimated Burden of Disease by Cause and Region, 1998

due to communicable disease is said to be roughly comparable. (Not surprisingly, China's per-capita DALY is still substantially higher than that computed for high-income Western countries, as is its estimated burden of infectious and parasitic disease.)

Table 4.2 presents the WHO's 1998 per-capita DALY estimates for infectious and parasitic disease from Figure 4.2 in greater detail. In absolute terms, in this calculus, the overall burden of infectious and parasitic disease is said to be about seven times as high in India as in China, and about a fifth lower in Low- and Middle-Income Europe. On a per-capita basis, by these calculations, the top five infectious and parasitic diseases result in about one-third more DALYs in post-communist Europe than in China—and about seven times more in India.

To judge by these WHO calculations, contemporary China has made very significant progress in suppressing communicable disease and has attained a health profile with respect to infectious and parasitic illnesses that is unusually favorable for a country of its income level. If the WHO figures are roughly accurate, indeed, China's current infectious disease profile might be likened to that of the European region: with a burden of communicable illness somewhere between that of Western and Eastern Europe.

We must remember that, in an important sense, China is an arithmetic average of disparate components—and those disparities also appear in the realm of health. Figure 4.3 makes the point: It outlines the provincial distribution of life expectancy for the Chinese population as of 1982, as estimated from the 1982 Chinese Census.[16] (Perhaps surprisingly, little in the way of research has been done on

---

[16]Data derived from Judith Banister, *China's Changing Population*, Stanford, Calif.: Stanford University Press, 1987; and Hongsheng Hao, Eduardo Arriaga, and Judith Banister, "China: Provincial Patterns of Mortality," paper presented at the Seminar on Mortality and Morbidity in South and East Asia, Beijing, August 29–September 2, 1988.

Table 4.2

WHO-Estimated Burden of Infectious and Parasitic Diseases by Cause and Region, 1998

Disease	China		India		High-Income WHO Member States		Low- and Middle-Income Europe	
	Thousands of DALYs Per Capita	% of Total DALYs by Cause	Thousands of DALYs Per Capita	% of Total DALYs by Cause	Thousands of DALYs Per Capita	% of Total DALYs by Cause	Thousands of DALYs Per Capita	% of Total DALYs by Cause
Infectious and parasitic diseases	9.6	5.8	68.8	25.1	3.3	2.8	12.1	6.3
Tuberculosis	3.1	1.9	7.7	2.8	0.1	0.1	1.8	0.9
STDs excluding HIV	0.1	0.1	5.0	1.8	0.5	0.4	1.1	0.6
HIV/AIDS	0.2	0.1	5.7	2.1	1.1	0.9	0.3	0.2
Diarrheal diseases	2.0	1.2	22.4	8.2	0.4	0.3	4.3	2.2
Childhood diseases	0.9	0.5	14.7	5.4	0.5	0.4	2.5	1.3
Meningitis	0.7	0.4	1.2	0.4	0.1	0.1	0.5	0.3
Hepatitis	0.4	0.2	0.3	0.1	0.1	0.1	0.2	0.1
Malaria	0.0	0.0	0.6	0.2	0.0	0.0	0.0	0.0
Tropical diseases	0.2	0.1	3.3	1.2	0.0	0.0	0.1	0.1
Leprosy	0.0	0.0	0.2	0.1	0.0	0.0	0.0	0.0
Dengue	0.0	0.0	0.4	0.1	0.0	0.0	0.0	0.0
Japanese encephalitis	0.3	0.2	0.1	0.0	0.0	0.0	0.0	0.0
Trachoma	0.3	0.2	0.0	0.0	0.0	0.0	0.2	0.1
Intestinal nematode infections	0.9	0.5	0.8	0.3	0.0	0.0	0.1	0.0
Other infectious diseases	0.6	0.3	6.4	2.4	0.5	0.4	1.0	0.5

SOURCE: World Health Organization, *The World Health Report 1999*, Geneva, Annex Table 3.

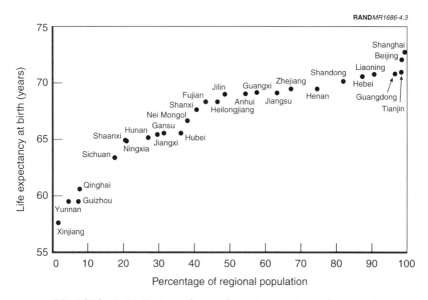

SOURCES: Judith Banister, *China's Changing Population*, Stanford, Calif.: Stanford University Press, 1987; Hongsheng Hao, Eduardo Arriaga, and Judith Banister, "China: Provincial Patterns of Mortality," paper presented at the Seminar on Mortality and Morbidity in South and East Asia, Beijing, August 29–September 2, 1988.

Figure 4.3—Percentage of Regional Populations by Life Expectancy: China, 1982

overall mortality disparities in China for more recent years;[17] nonetheless, though the specific numbers in Figure 4.3 are by now somewhat outdated, the general patterns highlighted still prevail.)

As of 1982, China's healthiest region (Shanghai) is thought to have enjoyed a life expectancy at birth roughly 15 years higher than its

_____

[17]One exception is Hongsheng Hao, "Trends and Geographic Differentials in Mortality," in Xizhe Peng, with Zhigang Guo, eds., *The Changing Population of China*, Malden, Mass.: Blackwell Publishers, 2000, pp. 34–50, which estimates provincial life expectancy on the basis of the 1990 Chinese Census. Official data on provincial life expectancies are available from Chinese statistical compendia; but those figures are not thought to make adequate adjustments for underreported mortality.

least healthy province (Xinjiang). (Note that Tibet is excluded from the calculations in Figure 4.3.) In regions accounting for roughly a fifth of China's total population, life expectancy then was 70 or higher; in another fifth, it was 65 or lower. Generally speaking (to go by the proxy of life expectancy) the health situation was best in the country's major municipalities and along the coast; overall health conditions were poorer in the inland provinces—and in more rural regions.

It would be reasonable to assume that the distribution of the communicable disease problem in China follows the same general pattern: In other words, we may presume that the current risk of epidemic, infectious, and parasitic disease is distinctly higher for the hundreds of millions of Chinese in rural regions or inland areas than it is for those in urban centers and coastal zones.

PROSPECTS FOR EPIDEMIC DISEASE IN CONTEMPORARY CHINA: THE RISKS OF BEHAVIOR-BORNE COMMUNICABLE ILLNESSES

China's health situation today is by no means ideal. Serious problems with infectious disease (most notably tuberculosis, which reportedly still claims 250,000 lives a year in contemporary China) assuredly persist.[18] The extensive if rudimentary socialized health care system of the Maoist era has given way, under the Deng era's economic reorientation, to a system that is largely pay for service, and full of coverage gaps, especially in rural areas.[19] With the aging of China's population, moreover, the question of how to finance medi-

---

[18]*Xinhua*, April 1, 2000, reprinted as "China Conducts TB Epidemiological Survey," FBIS-CHI-2000-0401, April 1, 2000; *Xinhua*, March 19, 1999, reprinted as "Ministry: 250,000 Die Annually from Tuberculosis," FBIS-CHI-1999-0319, March 19, 1999; *Xinhua*, March 25, 1998, reprinted as "China: New Hepatitis Virus Confirmed in China," FBIS-TEN-98-084, March 25, 1998; and *Xinhua*, April 7, 1997, reprinted as "CHINA: Official on Prevention, Treatment of Diseases," FBIS-TEN-97-004, April 7, 1997.

[19]See, for example, Marilyn Beach, "China's Rural Health Care Gradually Worsens," *Lancet*, Vol. 358, August 18, 2001, p. 567; Gerald Bloom and Shenglan Tang, "Rural Health Prepayment Schemes in China: Towards a More Active Role for Government," *Social Science and Medicine*, Vol. 48, No. 7, April 1999, pp. 951–960; and World Bank, *China: Long-Term Issues and Options in the Health Transition*, Washington, D.C.: World Bank, 1992.

cal treatment for chronic conditions and diseases of the elderly—largely unresolved today—will become increasingly pressing.[20]

For all those shortcomings, however, China's public health performance must be recognized for what it is: an unusually far-reaching achievement for a country with such a low level of per-capita income. Whatever the limitations of the Chinese public health apparatus, furthermore, China has clearly been able to control and gradually suppress the sorts of epidemic, infectious, and parasitic diseases that had afflicted its populace so sorely in earlier times. China appears to have a fairly workable model in place for dealing with waterborne, airborne, and food-borne infections.

Consequently, to posit a devastating upsurge of traditional infectious and parasitic illnesses (e.g., tuberculosis, influenza, hepatitis, malaria, meningitis, and the like) in China in the years ahead would seem to require the presumption that the mechanisms that have until now brought those afflictions so largely under control in contemporary China would suddenly suffer a systematic breakdown.

A public health disaster in China could surely follow a major systemic dislocation—for example, a collapse of central administrative authority, attended by a neglect of public health capabilities and an economic upheaval. But such a hypothetical public health disaster would be entirely contingent upon exogenous political shock—and although the unleashed health troubles might contribute to the country's consequent economic woes, they would simply be a "second-order effect."

Yet China's quite impressive record to date in checking epidemics and communicable diseases does not necessarily mean that newly emerging epidemics will be handled with equal efficacy under conditions of continuing political order. For the epidemic threats looming on the Chinese public health horizon look to be *behavior borne*, and behavior-borne epidemic disease may be more difficult for the Chinese health system to contain. The primary behavior-borne epi-

---

[20]See World Bank, *Financing Health Care: Issues and Options for China*, Washington, D.C.: World Bank, 1997.

demic threat on the horizon today is, of course, HIV/AIDS (human immunodeficiency virus/acquired immunodeficiency syndrome).[21]

As is well known by now, HIV/AIDS is principally transmitted through human-to-human body fluid transfer (principally by blood, through sexual contact or intravenous exchange, although it may also be transmitted to infant in utero or through breast-feeding). A lentivirus (i.e., slow gestating virus), HIV gradually destroys its human host's immunosystem, so that the victim succumbs to an ultimately lethal bout of any of a number of opportunistic diseases. At this writing, there is no known cure for HIV/AIDS—nor has research for an effective preventive vaccine as yet yielded practical results.

The literature on the HIV/AIDS problem in China is by now immense.[22] To summarize briefly the state of knowledge about the

---

[21]For a brief exposition on why behavior-driven epidemics may be intrinsically more difficult to control than "traditional" epidemics, see John C. Caldwell, "Rethinking the African AIDS Epidemic," *Population and Development Review*, Vol. 26, No. 1, March 2000, pp. 117–135.

The analysis in this chapter proceeds on the assumption that HIV/AIDS is and will remain the primary infectious disease threat to public health in China over the next decade and a half. Implicit in this assumption are two subsidiary presumptions: (1) that a medical breakthrough leading to an inexpensive cure for HIV/AIDS will not take place in the period under consideration; and (2) that a hitherto unknown infectious disease will not displace HIV/AIDS in terms of lethal potential in the coming decade and a half.

[22]For a sample of background materials from the press and more specialized journals, see Nicholas Eberstadt, "The Future of AIDS," *Foreign Affairs*, Vol. 80, No. 6, November/December 2002, pp. 21–45; U.S. National Intelligence Council, *The Next Wave of HIV/AIDS: Nigeria, Ethiopia, Russia, India, and China*, Washington, D.C.: NTIS, September 2002, ICA 2002-042; David Murphy, "AIDS: A Nightmare in the Making," *Far Eastern Economic Review*, August 15, 2002; UN Theme Group on HIV/AIDS in China, "HIV/AIDS: China's Titanic Peril," June 2002, www.unaids.org/whatsnew/newadds/AIDSChina_2001update.pdf, accessed June 30, 2002; Joan Kaufman and Jun Jing, "China and AIDS—The Time to Act Is Now," *Science*, Vol. 296, June 28, 2002, pp. 2339–2340; Elisabeth Rosenthal, "U.N. Publicly Chastises China for Inaction on HIV Epidemic," *The New York Times*, June 28, 2002; K. Zhang and S. Ma, "Epidemiology of HIV in China," *British Medical Journal*, Vol. 324, April 6, 2002, pp. 803–804; Bates Gill, Jennifer Chang, and Sarah Palmer, "China's HIV Crisis," *Foreign Affairs*, Vol. 81, No. 2, March/April 2002, pp. 96–110; Joint United Nations Programme on HIV/AIDS (hereafter, UNAIDS), *AIDS Epidemic Update: December 2001*, www.unaids.org/worldaidsday/2001/Epiupdate2001/Epiupdate2001_en.pdf, accessed December 10, 2001; Marilyn Beach, "China Responds to Increasing HIV/AIDS Burden and Holds Landmark Meeting," *The Lancet*, Vol. 358, November 24, 2001, p. 1792; Elisabeth Rosenthal, "AIDS Patients in China Lack Effective Treatment," *The New York Times*, November 1, 2001, p. A1; Elisabeth Rosenthal, "China Asks U.S. Agency to Help

current status of the epidemic in China: Because the overwhelming majority of HIV cases in the country are undocumented and un-treated, figures on the current prevalence (total cases) and incidence (new cases) of HIV among China's roughly 1.3 billion people rely heavily upon guesswork. In August 2001, Beijing health authorities announced that 600,000 Chinese were HIV-positive as of the year 2000. A little later, in July 2002, UNAIDS (i.e., the Joint United Na-tions Programme on HIV/AIDS) put the total number of people living with HIV/AIDS in China at 850,000—a figure with which Beijing, at the time, concurred. Just two months thereafter, in September 2002,

---

Combat H.I.V. Epidemic," *The New York Times*, August 31, 2001, p. A3; Bates Gill and Sarah Palmer, "The Coming AIDS Crisis in China," *The New York Times*, July 16, 2001, p. A15; Philip P. Pan, "Children's Lawsuits Force China to Confront AIDS," *Washington Post*, July 7, 2001, p. A1; John Pomfret, "Chinese City Is First to Enact Law on AIDS; Controversial Rule Set for Infected People, High-Risk Groups," *Washington Post*, January 15, 2001, p. A16; John Pomfret, "The High Cost of Selling Blood," *Washington Post*, January 11, 2001, p. A1; Abu Saleh M Abdullah, "Spread of HIV and AIDS in China," *The Lancet*, Vol. 356, November 25, 2000, p. 1856; Khabir Ahmad, "China Contemplates Criminalization of HIV Transmission," *The Lancet*, Vol. 356, November 11, 2000, p. 1666; Elisabeth Rosenthal, "In Rural China, a Steep Price of Poverty: Dying of AIDS," *The New York Times*, October 28, 2000, p. A1; "STD Rate Soars in China; Three in Four New Cases Are Among the Unmarried," *International Family Planning Perspectives*, Vol. 26, No. 3, September 2000, pp. 141–142; Elisabeth Rosenthal, "Scientists Warn of Inaction as AIDS Spreads in China," *The New York Times*, August 2, 2000, p. A1; Dennis Normile, "China Awakens to Fight Projected AIDS Crisis," *Science*, Vol. 288, June 30, 2000, pp. 2–3; UNAIDS, *China: Epidemiological Fact Sheet on HIV/AIDS and Sexually Transmitted Infections—2000 Update*, www.unaids.org/statistics/fact_sheets/pdfs/China_en.pdf, accessed July 10, 2000; AFP (Hong Kong), June 21, 2000, reprinted as "AFP: Prostitution, AIDS Said 'Rampant' in China," FBIS-CHI-2000-0621, June 21, 2000; Myron S. Cohen et al., "Sexually Transmitted Diseases in the People's Republic of China in Y2K: Back to the Future," *Sexually Transmitted Diseases*, Vol. 27, No. 3, March 2000, pp. 143–145; Y. Wang, "A Strategy of Clinical Tolerance for the Prevention of HIV and AIDS in China," *Journal of Medicine and Philosophy*, Vol. 25, No. 1, February 2000, pp. 48–61; AFP (Hong Kong), December 1, 1999, reprinted as "AFP: PRC Marks World AIDS Day with Condom Publicity Ban," FBIS-CHI-1999-1201, December 1, 1999; K. Zhang et al., "Changing Sexual Attitudes and Behavior in China: Implications for the Spread of HIV and Other Sexually Transmitted Diseases," *AIDS CARE*, Vol. 11, No. 5, October 1999, pp. 581–589; *Xinhua*, November 30, 1998, reprinted as "China: China Announces 12-Year Program of AIDS Control," FBIS-TEN-98-334, November 30, 1998; Richard Tomlinson, "China Recognizes AIDS Problem," *British Medical Journal*, Vol. 316, February 14, 1998, p. 493; Elena S. H. Yu et al., "HIV Infection in China, 1985 Through 1994," *American Journal of Public Health*, Vol. 86, No. 8, August 1996, pp. 1116–1122; and Qin Shulin et al., "First Case of Sexual Transmission of Human Immunodeficiency Virus in Mainland China," *Proceedings of the Chinese Academy of Medical Sciences and the Peking University Medical College*, Vol. 4, No. 4, December 1989, pp. 235–236.

the head of the Chinese Health Ministry's Department of Disease Control raised the official estimate to one million.

Other sources, however, suggest the total may be higher—perhaps far higher. (According to some claims, indeed, the province of Henan alone might already have 1.2 million or more HIV carriers.) A June 2002 report by the UN Theme Group on HIV/AIDS in China suggested that a reasonable estimate for China's 2001 HIV population was 800,000 to 1,500,000. The U.S. intelligence community, for its part, places China's year 2002 HIV-positive population at 1 million to 2 million. Nor is this the upper boundary of informed guesswork. In June 2002, an unnamed UN official told *The New York Times* that there certainly could be as many as 6 million HIV cases in China; if that surmise proved accurate, China might have the largest HIV population of any country in the world.

But whatever the true current rate of HIV prevalence in China may be, there is little doubt that totals are rising very, very swiftly. Chinese authorities and UNAIDS, for instance, both suggest that the prevalence of HIV in China has been increasing by about 20–30 percent per annum in recent years; the U.S. Centers for Disease Control and Prevention (CDC), for its part, cites estimates of a current "doubling time" of 30 months.

It is thought that HIV is currently transmitted in China by three main routes: (1) through extramarital heterosexual intercourse (abetted by the ongoing expansion of China's commercial sex business); (2) through illicit intravenous (IV) drug use; and (3) through the unsafe sale of blood (a procedure that can infect both recipients and vendors). To date, the Chinese HIV epidemic appears to be predominantly heterosexual in disposition, and the risk of HIV in China appears to be disproportionately high among the poor, the uneducated, and the rural. Current high-risk subpopulations are believed to include IV drug-users, persons selling (or using purchased) blood, and persons active in the commercial sex network. Larger at-risk groups may include the so-called "floating population" (the 100 million or more unauthorized migrants from rural regions seeking opportunity on the fringes of Chinese urban life) and the "unmarriageable males" (the rising numbers of young men in China who, due to the country's growing youth gender imbalance, have no realistic prospect of securing a bride).[23]

At this juncture, it seems very likely that China's HIV/AIDS problem will worsen considerably in the years ahead—in part because of choices made by Chinese policymakers, in part because of the limited options open to them.

To date, the Chinese government's response to its mounting HIV crisis has been piecemeal—but important components of that response have involved the segregation of HIV carriers, or the proposed criminal prosecution of HIV sufferers for the very activities that resulted in HIV infection. This draconian approach naturally encourages HIV carriers to avoid detection and to misrepresent their health status, thereby fueling further spread of the epidemic. Beijing has also attempted to suppress public discussion of the "tainted blood" problem, arresting activists working on the HIV commercial blood sales issue and shutting down their web sites. (Chinese authorities may be uneasy about the government's arguable complicity in fomenting this aspect of the national HIV problem.) From an epidemiological standpoint, of course, such strictures are at best utterly ineffective: for an epidemic cannot be censored.

In contemporary Asia, perhaps the most successful HIV-control campaign thus far has been that of Thailand. Whether China could replicate a Thailand-style anti-AIDS policy is by no means clear. Analyses of the Thai program by the World Bank[24] and other groups have stressed the important role of "civil society" in the Thai strategy: Nongovernmental organizations assumed a major role in the prevention campaign, and popular trust in the government apparently lent credibility to the state's massive public education effort. A public health campaign premised upon the independence of nonstate actors and the population's confidence in its government could be rather more problematic for Beijing.

---

[23]See "6.3 Brides for Seven Brothers," *The Economist*, Vol. 349, December 19, 1998, pp. 56–58; Nicholas Eberstadt, *Prosperous Paupers and Other Population Problems*, New Brunswick, N.J.: Transaction Publishers, 2000, Chapter 10.

[24]"Thailand's Response to AIDS: Building on Success, Confronting the Future," *Thailand Social Monitor* (World Bank), No. V, November 2000, www.worldbank.or.th/cgi-bin/load?social/pdf/Thailand's%20Response%20AIDS.pdf, accessed January 28, 2002.

In any case, it is worth noting, Thailand's ostensibly exemplary AIDS campaign did not immediately check the spread of the epidemic. As Figure 4.4 underscores, by UNAIDS' reckoning, Thailand's HIV-positive population continued to increase for about a decade after the implementation of the country's aggressive anti-AIDS strategy, almost tripling over the interim.

China's response to its HIV crisis may also be circumscribed by economic considerations. Not the least of these concern the "net present value" of treatment for HIV carriers. For now, the most effective medical intervention for prolonging HIV patients' lives is the so-called Highly Active Anti-Retroviral Therapy (HAART, or "drug cocktail" regimen). The HAART regimen appears to extend the AIDS-free life expectancy of HIV patients by several years, thereby permitting

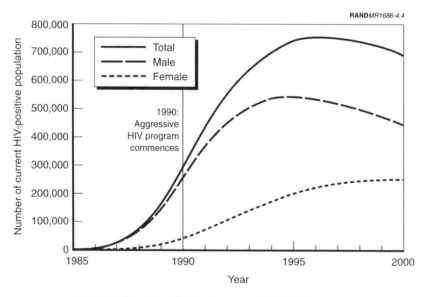

SOURCE: The Thai Working Group on HIV/AIDS Projection, *Projections for HIV/AIDS in Thailand: 2000–2020*, Bangkok, Thailand, February 2001.

Figure 4.4—Anatomy of a "Success": Estimated HIV Prevalence in Thailand, 1985–2000

continued work for the economically active. The cost-benefit calculus of the HAART regimen, however, is quite unforgiving for low-income populations.

In the West, where proprietary medicines are used, the HAART treatment is very expensive—typically $10,000 or more per patient per year. The generic versions of those medicines cost much less: In India, for example, the pharmaceutical manufacturer Cipla Ltd. currently markets a year's supply of HAART medications for about $600. Yet as the illustrative calculations in Figure 4.5 attest, even at tremendously discounted prices, HAART would not necessarily prove to be an economic bargain for treating HIV-afflicted workers in low-income countries.

Under the arbitrary but not unreasonable assumptions outlined in Figure 4.5, the "social benefit" (through extended work life) of providing workers with generic HAART medications would only outweigh the "social cost" for laborers with an annual output of several thousand dollars a year. Even if HAART treatments could be obtained for free and dispensed only at the cost of the limited medical supervision entailed, workers generating much less than $1,000 per annum would not be able to produce as much additional output for their society as their treatment would absorb in resource costs.[25]

There are, to be sure, consequential differences in estimated output per worker in China, depending upon whether one relies upon exchange-rate-based comparisons or the alternative "purchasing-power-parity" (PPP) techniques.[26] Irrespective of the approach that

---

[25]The situation may be even less promising than this analysis suggests. In order for the HAART therapy to be effective, the regimen must be followed quite closely, pursued in some instances literally on an hour-by-hour basis. It follows that implementing the regimen requires a sophisticated medical infrastructure—and very possibly, intensive utilization of its resources. Whether China's health care system could meet these challenges is a critical question—and the answer is not self-evidently "yes." If the answer is in the affirmative, moreover, the question of health service costs then arises: If actual costs are substantially higher than we have hypothesized, the entire cost-benefit calculus shifts, and in a direction inauspicious for China's at-risk groups.

[26]For a review of the issues and results, see Angus Maddison, *Chinese Economic Performance in the Long Run*, Paris: OECD, 1998; Alan Heston, "PPP Comparisons in the ESCAP Region: What Have We Learned?" paper prepared for symposium on Statistical Measurement of Economic Development of China and East Asian Region, Institute of

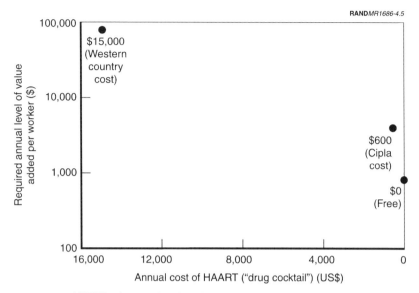

RANDMR1686-4.5

NOTES: Assumptions in calculations:
- Discount rate of 10 percent per year
- Average HAART treatment begins four years after HIV infection
- Life expectancy after onset of AIDS averages two years
- HAART treatment extends healthy life an average of three years
- Administering HAART requires $150 per year in health care services
- Worker output fixed—unchanged by infection
- Worker ceases gainful employment with onset of AIDS.

Figure 4.5—Average Levels of Annual Worker Output Required to Pay for HAART Treatment: Illustrative Calculations

one ultimately deems appropriate for estimating output per worker in contemporary China, it will be apparent that a consequential pro-

International Studies, Meiji Gakuin University, Yokohama, Japan, November 19, 2000, www.meijigakuin.ac.jp/~iism/pdf/nonpo_003/Heston.pdf, accessed January 29, 2002; and Richard N. Cooper, "Chinese Economic and Budgetary Prospects," testimony before the U.S.-China Commission, December 7, 2001, www.uscc.gov/tescpr.htm, accessed January 30, 2002.

portion of the population at risk of contracting HIV/AIDS in China today would not qualify as candidates for HAART therapy on the basis of social cost-benefit calculations per se.

MODELING POSSIBLE TRAJECTORIES FOR AN HIV EPIDEMIC IN CHINA

Tremendous uncertainties attend the attempt to model the future of the HIV/AIDS epidemic. Public health specialists and epidemiologists have not yet developed robust techniques to permit them to predict the unfolding course of the epidemic with any degree of precision; in large measure, they still lack even the detailed epidemiological data that would allow them to explain convincingly the mechanisms of HIV transmission within ostensibly heterosexual low-income populations.

Those same uncertainties weigh heavily on any effort to project possible trajectories for the HIV/AIDS epidemic in China in the years ahead. Given those considerable constraints, we cannot presume to predict the future course of China's HIV/AIDS epidemic. We can, however, illustrate the likely demographic outcomes that would devolve from a range of explicitly specified and carefully described HIV scenarios, utilizing demographic and epidemiological modeling techniques.

What is important to keep in mind in this exercise is that the modeled assumptions drive the results. Table 4.3 lays out those assumptions and inputs for the reader.

In this exercise we relied upon the "SPECTRUM" demographic-epidemiological software package[27] and set as our Chinese demographic "baseline" the U.S. Census Bureau's 2000–2025 projections for China from its international database (October 2002 revisions).

---

[27]Developed by The Futures Group International for the U.S. Agency for International Development, www.tfgi.com/spectrum.exe.

Table 4.3

China HIV/AIDS Epidemic Modeling Parameters

AIDS epidemic modeled with SPECTRUM software assuming
1. AIDS epidemic began in 1985 in China
2. Median AIDS incubation period of nine years
3. Life expectancy after AIDS of two years
4. Standard "heterosexual" distribution structure

Six initial scenarios
1. Order of magnitude increase
    (Between 2000 and 2025, HIV prevalence rises from 0.14% to 4.0%)
2. Stabilized epidemic
    (HIV prevalence rises by 2015 to 3.5% then holds steady until 2025)
3. Mitigated epidemic
    (Same as scenario 2 up to 2015; thereafter, HIV prevalence declines by 2025 to
    2.0%)
4. Really bad epidemic
    (By 2025, 9.0% for China)
5. Mild epidemic
    (HIV prevalence rises by 2015 to 1.5% then holds steady until 2025)
6. Very mild epidemic
    (Same as scenario 5 up to 2015; thereafter, HIV prevalence declines by 2025 to
    1.0%)

SOURCE: U.S. Census Bureau, *Baseline Age Structure, Fertility/Mortality/Migration Assumptions: U.S. Census Bureau International Database Projections, 2000–2025.*

In our scenarios, we modeled six hypothetical trajectories for the HIV/AIDS epidemic in China over the period 2000–2025. For midyear 2002, we assumed that the prevalence of HIV among China's "adult" population (ages 15–49) was 0.28 percent. (We were assuming a total HIV-positive population for China of just over 2 million.) We further assumed that the true HIV prevalence figure for 2000 was 1 million, or about 0.14 percent adult prevalence. These numbers are higher than the ones currently accepted by Beijing—but Beijing's preferred numbers may very well prove to be underestimates.

The prevalence curves for the six separate HIV scenarios (see Table 4.3) are traced out in Figure 4.6.

How realistic are the assumptions embodied in these six scenarios? One way of putting those hypothetical trajectories in perspective is to compare them with existing projections and existing estimates of HIV prevalence for other countries or regions.

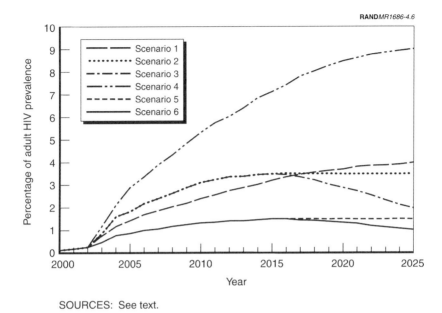

SOURCES: See text.

Figure 4.6—China Prevalence Curves: Six Scenarios

Only one of our scenarios (i.e., "Really Bad Epidemic") posits an eventual adult HIV prevalence rate as high as those in the so-called "Low Scenario" modeled by the U.S. Census to describe possible future HIV paths for urban Africa.[28] The 9 percent adult HIV prevalence rate that the "Really Bad Epidemic" ascribes to China in the year 2025 can be further compared against UNAIDS' estimate of a sub-Sahara-wide prevalence rate of 8.8 percent for year-end 2002.

Of the five remaining scenarios only one ("Order of Magnitude Increase") posits an eventual adult HIV prevalence rate as high as that estimated by UNAIDS for Cambodia as of year-end 1999 (i.e., 4 percent). And in two of the scenarios ("Mild Epidemic" and "Very Mild Epidemic"), the prevalence rates presumed for China's HIV epidemic

---

[28]U.S. Bureau of the Census, *World Population Profile: 1998*, Washington, D.C.: U.S. Census Bureau International Programs Center, 1999, Table B-1.

never reach the levels estimated to characterize contemporary Thailand (i.e., 2 percent).[29]

Inescapably and necessarily, every one of these scenarios is speculative. The actual trajectory of China's HIV epidemic in the years ahead will be established by patterns and mechanisms of transmission, the prevalence of risky behaviors and practices among the general public, and the efficacy of the government's anti-AIDS strategies—quantities we cannot know today. From our present-day vantage point, however, each of these six scenarios can be seen to comport with HIV prevalence rates well within the contemporary historical experience of other societies (and in five of the six scenarios, within the historical experience of nearby East Asian societies). In that respect, none of these scenarios would appear to be prima facie implausible.

What would these various HIV trajectories suggest about the unfolding of the AIDS epidemic in China in the years immediately ahead? We may begin by considering the implications for the size of the total HIV-positive population (see Figure 4.7). Under our most "pessimistic" trajectory, China would have almost 80 million HIV carriers by the year 2025; under our most "optimistic" scenario, that number would "only" be about 11 million. Looking to the medium term—that is, to the year 2015—the "optimistic" trajectories posit a total HIV-positive Chinese population of about 14 million and the "pessimistic," a total of over 60 million, with the intermediate trajectories centering around 30 million.

The curves in Figure 4.7 are of course derived directly from the HIV prevalence scenarios from Figure 4.6. If the underlying assumptions guiding these scenarios are plausible, however, the numbers in Figure 4.7 suggest that China could soon have a far larger HIV-positive population than that found in any country in the world to date. *In fact, in four of the six scenarios in Figure 4.7, China's HIV population in the year 2015 would approach or exceed the entire estimated HIV population of sub-Saharan Africa today.*

---

[29]Year-end 1999 adult HIV prevalence rates in the preceding paragraphs drawn from UNAIDS, *Report on the Global HIV/AIDS Epidemic: June 2000*, www.unaids.org/epidemic_update/report/Epi_report.pdf, accessed January 31, 2002.

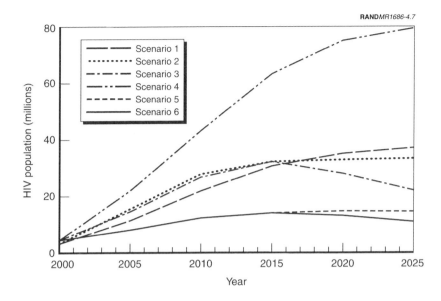

Figure 4.7—Projected HIV Population: China, 2000–2025

Until a cure for AIDS is discovered, HIV will continue to be invariably fatal. Table 4.4 charts the cumulative AIDS deaths implied for China under the six separate scenarios modeled above. Our model posits that China had only suffered about 20,000 AIDS deaths as of the year 2000 (quite possibly, a low estimate). But given the cruel arithmetic of the epidemic, those totals explode in every one of our scenarios.

By 2010, every one of our scenarios imputes a cumulative total of roughly 4 million or more AIDS deaths to China: The "pessimistic" trajectory implies about 12 million, and the intermediate trajectories are about 8 million. By the year 2015, our scenarios imply a cumulative total of 10–37 million AIDS deaths for China. Put another way, our China scenarios envision average AIDS deaths for the years 2010–2015 of 1.2 million per year on the low side and about 5 million a year on the high side. (To put those numbers in perspective, the U.S. Census Bureau estimates China's total mortality in the year 2000 to be just under 9 million.)

Table 4.4

China's Cumulative AIDS Deaths
(in millions)

	2000	2005	2010	2015	2020	2025
Scenario 1	0.02	0.44	6.37	17.94	31.19	44.64
Scenario 2	0.02	0.46	8.07	22.89	37.04	48.27
Scenario 3	0.02	0.46	8.07	22.89	36.88	45.68
Scenario 4	0.02	0.51	11.90	37.24	67.00	96.81
Scenario 5	0.02	0.39	3.98	10.31	16.27	21.13
Scenario 6	0.02	0.39	3.98	10.31	16.23	20.46

By 2020–2025, under our most "pessimistic" HIV trajectory, China would be suffering almost 6 million AIDS deaths a year. By the arithmetic of the intermediate scenarios, annual AIDS deaths would total 2.2 million–2.6 million. Even under the "optimistic" trajectories, AIDS deaths would be mounting at a pace of over 800,000 per year. By 2025, cumulative AIDS mortality for China in every modeled scenario would exceed 20 million (or nearly the total number of deaths thought to have been experienced by all of humanity in the first two decades of the global HIV pandemic).

ECONOMIC IMPLICATIONS FOR CHINA OF HIV "BREAKOUT"

Under all of the scenarios modeled in the previous section, HIV in China would qualify as a humanitarian tragedy of unprecedented and devastating dimensions. But would such a tragedy have appreciable ramifications for China's economic performance?

The answer to the question may not be self-evident. Economies do not necessarily fare poorly during sudden, brutal bouts of mortality. During World War II, for example, the output levels of most of the major combatant powers increased significantly during the first years of hostilities, despite sharply increased death rates for persons of productive age.[30] More theoretically (and prosaically), the familiar

---

[30]See, for example, Alan S. Milward, *War, Economy and Society, 1939–1945*, Berkeley, Calif.: University of California Press, 1977.

"Lewis two-sector model" of economic development would suggest that loss of low-productivity population from the "traditional" sector would impose only minimal losses on the overall economy—and it is precisely those segments of Chinese society that seem at disproportionate HIV risk at present.

To date, relatively little research has been devoted to the macroeconomic implications of HIV/AIDS—and most of that work has focused on the sub-Saharan region.[31] The current state of economic thinking about this complex set of far-reaching interactions might fairly be described as introductory and exploratory. While this emerging literature has identified such issues as the potential effect of AIDS-increased mortality on population growth, labor supply, "dependency ratios," and savings rates, many other possible factors bearing on long-run economic performance have not been seriously discussed.

In particular, two important potential economic ramifications of an HIV/AIDS epidemic in a low-income setting have as yet received little attention. First, by foreshortening adult life spans, a widespread HIV epidemic would seriously alter the calculus of investment in higher education and technical skills—thereby undermining the local process of investment in human capital. Second, widespread HIV prevalence could affect international decisions about direct investment, technical transfer, and managerial encampment in locales perceived to be of high health risk. In these fashions, HIV "breakout" could have far-reaching economic consequences—in effect, driving a wedge between the countries afflicted and the ongoing economic process of "globalization." It is possible to imagine that the long-run economic impact of these HIV/AIDS effects could potentially be even more significant than the constraints the epidemic could impose on supplies of labor and/or local savings.

---

[31]For example, see David E. Bloom and Ajay S. Mahal, "Does the AIDS Epidemic Threaten Economic Growth," *Journal of Econometrics*, Vol. 77, No. 1, March 1997, pp. 105–124; Channing Arndt and Jeffrey D. Lewis, "The Macro Implications of HIV/AIDS in South Africa: A Preliminary Assessment," *South African Journal of Economics*, Vol. 68, No. 5, December 2000, pp. 856–887; Malcolm F. McPherson in association with Deborah A. Hoover and Donald R. Snodgrass, "The Impact on Economic Growth in Africa of Rising Costs and Labor Productivity Losses Associated with HIV/AIDS," Cambridge, Mass.: John F. Kennedy School of Government, Harvard University, unpublished paper.

From a technical standpoint, a precise calculation of the prospective economic cost of HIV/AIDS for a given society would be an extraordinarily exacting task. In effect, it would require an accurate estimation of the net present value of the diminution in the current population's income stream and the net present value of the increase in its consumption of HIV-related goods and services. Such a project may be beyond our reach for some time to come.

On the other hand, one very simple but nonetheless instructive way of thinking about the possible economic implications of an HIV "breakout" in China would be in terms of a "health-based productivity model." In modern times, there has been a robust correspondence between health and productivity at the national level. This association holds both across nations at any given point in time, and also within particular countries over time. A simple regression plotting World Bank estimates of per-capita output (PPP-adjusted GDP per capita) against estimated life expectancy at birth for 155 countries for the year 1999, for example, captures two-thirds of the variance in the data set (see Figure 4.8). By the same token, a simple regression of life expectancy and per-capita output in China for the period since 1963 (i.e., since the end of the Great Leap famine) captures over 70 percent of the variance in that data set (see Figure 4.9). In both the "snapshot" international data set and the longitudinal Chinese data set, simple regressions suggest that a single year's increase in life expectancy at birth is associated with an increase in per-capita output of about 8 percent.

These simple regressions, of course, do not capture the complexity of the health-productivity relationship, nor do they indicate causal directions. On the one hand, wealth is an instrument that helps households and populations to afford the consumption and lifestyle patterns that are conducive to healthier life.[32] On the other, improvements in health can boost productivity by extending potential work life, enhancing physical capacity, facilitating learning, and

---

[32]See Lant Pritchett and Lawrence H. Summers, "Wealthier Is Healthier," *Journal of Human Resources*, Vol. 31, No. 4, Fall 1996, pp. 841–868.

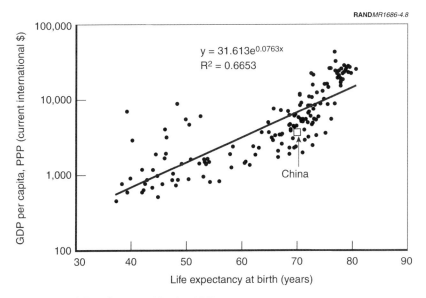

RAND*MR1686-4.8*

$$y = 31.613e^{0.0763x}$$
$$R^2 = 0.6653$$

China

Life expectancy at birth (years)

SOURCE: World Bank, 2000b.

Figure 4.8—GDP Per Capita for 155 Countries Versus Life Expectancy, 1999

contributing to "human capital deepening."[33] Yet while the interactions between health and productivity are manifestly intricate and multidirectional, the brute fact is that for any country, at any point in time, life expectancy can be trusted as a fairly good predictor of per-capita output.[34] That being the case, what would the scenarios from

---

[33]See Rati Ram and T. W. Schultz, "Life Span, Health, Savings and Productivity," *Economic Development and Cultural Change*, Vol. 27, No. 3, April 1979, pp. 399–421; Robert William Fogel, "New Findings on Secular Trends in Nutrition and Mortality: Some Implications for Population Theory," in Mark R. Rosenzweig and Oded Stark, eds., *Handbook of Population and Family Economics*, Volume 14, New York: Elsevier Sciences, 1997, pp. 433–481.

[34]According to the data in Figure 4.8, China is currently an "underperformer" in health-based predictions of per-capita output: Actual per-capita output, to go by World Bank estimates, was about 45 percent lower than life expectancy numbers would have suggested, ceteris paribus. But of course all other things were *not* equal—

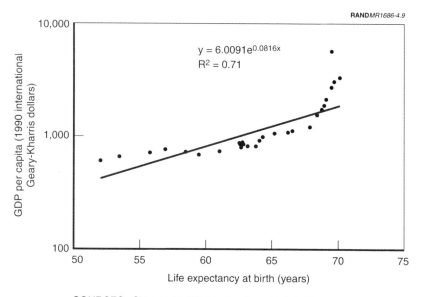

SOURCES: Sheng Luo, "Reconstruction of Life Tables and Age Distributions for the Population of China, by Year, from 1953 to 1982," New York: United Nations, World Population Prospects, 2000 revision; World Bank, 2000b; Angus Maddison, *The World Economy: A Millennial Perspective*, OECD, Paris, 2001, Table C3-c.

NOTES: Figures for 1963–1981 are from Luo and for 1982–1999 are from World Bank.

Figure 4.9—GDP Per Capita Versus Life Expectancy in China, 1963–1999

our China HIV models above augur for the country's prospective economic performance?

For "health-based productivity" predictions, we need to quantify HIV's impact on China's public health. Figure 4.10 does just that: It

---

and this is why China's relatively favorable endowment of human resources resulted in a relatively low level of output per capita in 1999. It should be no surprise to any observer to learn that contemporary China is an underperformer in this graphic. With a strengthening of the country's economic institutions (i.e., market order and rule of law), we would expect that China would move closer to the observed international association between health and output.

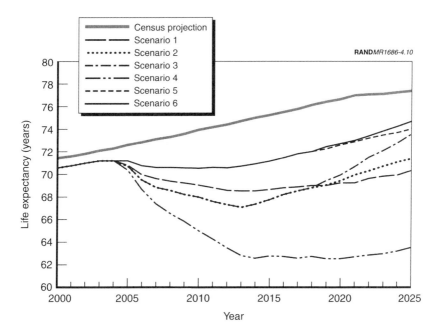

SOURCE: World Bank, 2001a; Luo, 2000 revision.

Figure 4.10—Projected Life Expectancy in China, 2000–2025

compares life expectancy at birth under the six HIV prevalence scenarios with our baseline projection for life expectancy in China over
the 2000–2025 period (assuming that HIV/AIDS does not otherwise
alter the endogenous improvements in life expectancy in China
posited in the Census Bureau "baseline" projections). As we see, all
of the HIV scenarios would alter China's anticipated trajectory of
health improvements over the coming generation.

In two of the six scenarios, life expectancy at birth in China would be
lower in 2025 than it is today. Conversely, under the most
"optimistic" of the scenarios, life expectancy in China in 2025 would
be "only" three years lower than the baseline projection.

The situation is, in some ways, even starker for the year 2015. For that year, four of the six scenarios imply a life expectancy lower than in the year 2002; in the other two scenarios, life expectancy in 2015 would be barely higher than it was 15 years earlier. In 2015, indeed, life expectancy under these six scenarios would be between 4 and 12 years lower than the "baseline" Census Bureau series would have projected.

Health-based predictions of output provide a very rough quantitative indication of the economic consequences of the HIV epidemics envisioned in these scenarios. If we assume that one year of improved life expectancy continues to be associated with about an 8 percent increase in per-capita GDP in the years ahead, the HIV epidemics hypothesized in this chapter would cut China's long-run (2000–2025) growth rate per person 15–64 years of age by about 0.5–0.7 percent per year in the "optimistic" scenarios, by over 3.5 percent per year in the most "pessimistic" scenario, and by 1.5–2.5 percent in the intermediate scenarios. For the year 2015, corresponding calculations imply reductions in per-capita growth rates ranging from 1.5 percent per annum to over 5 percent per annum, with "intermediate" scenarios exceeding 2.5 percent per annum.[35]

Clearly, all of those particular numbers are premised upon a number of major assumptions. The underlying point, however, is less open to contention: If health levels in China are severely affected by an HIV/AIDS epidemic and the country's health levels remain closely related to the country's economic potential, economic growth in China will suffer correspondingly. For these reasons, HIV/AIDS could indeed prove to be an exogenous factor—an independent "wild

---

[35]We should note that the health-based-productivity approach offers what would be taken as very low estimates of prospective productivity growth for China. Using Census Bureau projections as a baseline, they would imply a per-capita increase of just 1.9 percent per annum for 2000–2025—a pace much slower than that anticipated by most informed observers today (including the authors of other chapters in this volume). What should be noted here is that our crude method here is offering something like an estimate of the "independent" influence of the health effect. If China were to move away from its "outlier" status on the graphic in Figure 4.8 and up to the international curve traced out there (through improvements in economic institutions, etc.), a substantial increase in per-capita output would result. "Economic reforms" and "institutional reforms" in China over the generation under consideration would thus be consonant with a more rapid pace of growth than the one implied by our simple method alone.

card"—in the Chinese economic development process over the decades immediately ahead.

Chapter Five

WATER RESOURCES AND POLLUTION

Our analysis of China's complex water and pollution problems begins with estimates of the sharply differing water supply and demand conditions within China. The discussion then considers the economic effects of floods, water shortages, and pollution, concluding with an evaluation of alternative means and scenarios for addressing these problems and their respective costs and consequences.

ESTIMATING WATER SUPPLY AND DEMAND

Water Resources and Regional Disparities

Global water resources amount to 42,655 billion m^3, and global water resources per capita in 2000 were 7,045 m^3 (World Resource Institute [WRI] et al., 2000). China's water resources are huge, 2,812 billion m^3, which is 6.6 percent of the world total and the fourth largest in the world. However, China's population is very large; hence, the annual flow of per-capita water resources in 2000 is 2,201 m^3 (WRI et al., 2000)—less than one-third the world average. According to the WRI water-criticality classification framework, current nationwide water availability per capita in China is slightly above the sufficiency threshold level (Yang and Zehnder, 2001), although it will eventually approach the alarmingly low level of 1,700 m^3 per capita by 2030, when China's population will exceed 1.5 billion.

China's natural and socioeconomic conditions vary substantially, and China especially suffers a major imbalance in the timing[1] and location of its water supply. As shown in Figure 5.1, Yang and Zehnder (2001) illustrate the spatial distribution of water resources per capita (without considering water inflow and outflow) across provinces using the water-criticality classification, revealing a serious water shortage in the North China plain. Many rivers of the 3-H basins (Hai-Huai-Huang Rivers) are dry for five to eight months of the year. The Yellow (Huang) River, the cradle of Chinese civilization and the country's second longest river, with a drainage area of about 750,000 km^2, has annual runoff of less than 7 percent of that of the Yangtze River. The Yellow River has been overused, and since 1985, it has run dry each year; in 1997, it failed to reach the sea for 226 days. The inflows into Shandong dropped from 40 billion m^3 in the early 1980s to around 25 billion m^3 in the 1990s (Yang and Zehnder, 2001), and a similar situation is evident in Hebei and Henan as well. With growing upstream claims, the Yellow River may at some point no longer reach Shandong province at all.

The problem is not simply regional but also national, because the North China plain is one of the nation's key economic areas, holding one-third of the nation's population (424 million people), 40 percent of the cultivated land, and 31 percent of total GDP. This region has been the "breadbasket" of China, producing over 67 percent of the nation's wheat and 44 percent of its corn. However, the rivers of the northeast basins account for only 7.5 percent of the country's total runoff discharge (see Table 5.1). The water shortage is particularly serious in the Hai River basin which has a population of 92 million and includes the Beijing-Tianjin region.

Compared with the average water use shown in Table 5.2, the annual withdrawal per capita in the Hai River basin region cannot reach even the level of low-income countries without mining groundwater stock, transferring water across the basin, or recycling used water, even assuming that annually renewable water resources were completely allowed for. Groundwater has been tapped to make up the

---

[1]China has a typical monsoon climate, and precipitation mostly concentrates during the rainy season, which lasts a maximum of four months. This rainfall accounts for 50–80 percent of the annual rainfall.

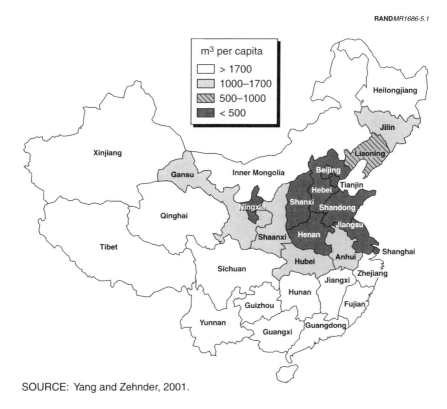

RAND*MR1686-5.1*

SOURCE: Yang and Zehnder, 2001.

Figure 5.1—Per-Capita Water Availability by Province, 1998

difference, resulting in overexploitation of subsurface water and ground subsidence, seawater intrusion, drying up of shallow aquifers, and falling water tables. The consequence of groundwater depletion is exhaustion and desertion of wells. In 1997, about 220,000 new wells were drilled, but at the same time, 100,000 old ones were deserted in the North China plain, and particularly in Beijing and Tianjin, the numbers of deserted wells exceeded those of newly drilled wells (Yang and Zehnder, 2001). Irrigation relying on overexploiting of groundwater stock is unsustainable, and the absolute decline that occurred in Beijing and Tianjin could occur in other provinces like Shandong and Hebei.

Table 5.1

Annually Renewable Water Resources in China, 1993

Region		Surface Runoff (billions of m³)	Ground-water (billions of m³)	Total Water Resources^a (billions of m³)	Water Resources (percentage)	Population (percent-age)	Cultivated Land (percent-age)	Per-Capita Water Resources (m³/yr/person)	Water Resources Per Crop Land (m³/yr/ha)
I	Northeastern	165.3	62.5	192.8	6.9	10	19.8	1,479	9,560
II	Hai He-Luan He basin	28.8	26.5	42.1	1.5	10	10.9	225	3,760
III	Huai He basin	74.1	39.3	96.1	3.4	16	14.9	389	6,310
IV	Huang He basin	66.1	40.6	74.4	2.6	8	12.7	656	5,730
	II+III+IV	169.0	106.4	212.6	7.5	34	38.5		
V	Yangtze River basin	951.3	246.4	961.3	34.2	34	24.0	2,369	39,300
VI	Southern	468.5	111.6	470.8	16.8	12	6.8	3,465	67,950
VII	Southeastern	255.7	61.3	259.2	9.2	6	3.2	2,999	73,800
VIII	Southwestern	585.3	154.4	585.3	20.8	2	1.7	31,679	327,000
	V+VI+VII+VIII	2,260.8	573.7	2,276.6	81.0	54	35.7		
IX	Interior basins	116.4	86.2	130.4	4.6	2	5.8	4,832	21,850
	National total	2,711.5	828.8	2,812.4	100.0	100.0	100.0	2,323	28,000

SOURCE: Feilig, 1999.

^aTotal water resources are less than surface runoff plus groundwater because of some double counting in the latter two sources.

Table 5.2

Water Withdrawals

Group	Annual Withdrawal Per Capita (m³)	Withdrawals by Sector (percentage)		
		Domestic	Industry	Agriculture
Low income	386	4	5	91
Middle income	453	13	18	69
High income	1,167	14	47	39
World (1995)	664	9	19	67
China (1993)	439	5	18	77

SOURCES: World Bank, 1994; World Resource Institute et al., 2000.

In addition, as growing wastewater discharges from the industrial and urban sectors exceed the capacity of treatment facilities, China's water shortage problems are aggravated by pollution. Since the volume of surface runoff is so small in North China, even a small amount of pollutant easily degrades water bodies below the quality level suitable for irrigation, and in turn, this pollution further aggravates the shortage of water resources. Figure 5.2 shows the trend of water quality in the seven main rivers in 1991 and 1998. The incidence of both good quality and poor quality increased during the 1990s in both North and South China. The incidence of class V/V+ (poor quality not even fit for irrigation) river water is three times higher in the north. In North China, while the Liao and Huai Rivers showed some improvement, conditions in the Hai, Yellow, and Songhua Rivers have deteriorated (World Bank, 2001b).

In sum, water shortages and pollution have become a serious limiting factor of the regional development of North China.

Demand Estimation for Agriculture, Industry, and Municipalities

China extracted 543.5 billion m³ of water in 1998, a 22 percent increase from 443.7 billion m³ in 1980. In 1993, total withdrawal was 518.7 billion m³ (see Table 5.3), and 78 percent of this water was used by agricultural sectors (66 percent for irrigation); industry was the second largest user, but urban water supply systems used only 24

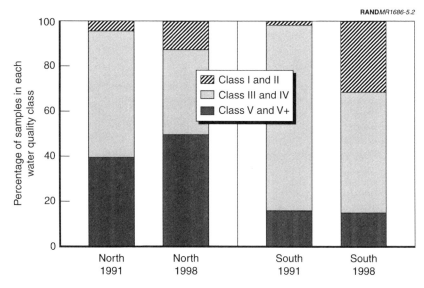

SOURCE: World Bank, 2001b.

NOTES: North China: 3-H, Songhua, and Liao Rivers; South China: Yangtze and Pearl Rivers.

Figure 5.2—Comparison of Water Quality in North and South China, 1991 and 1998

billion m^3. While agriculture is by far the dominant user, the growth in agricultural water use was very low—the increase between 1980 and 1993 was only 4 percent, despite increases in the area of irrigated fields, from 20.8 million hectares (ha) in 1985 to 22.5 million ha in 1995. By comparison, the increase in industrial water use was 94 percent, and urban water supply use increased remarkably by 256 percent, from 6.8 billion m^3 in 1980.

Domestic water consumption in urban areas has been rising due to both urbanization and increased per-capita consumption by urban residents (from 113 liters/day in 1980 to 230 liters/day in 1997). The highest share of urban water use was found in the Hai-Luan River basin, which includes Beijing and Tianjin (see Table 5.3).

Table 5.3

Water Use by Economic Sector in China, 1993
(billions of cubic meters)

Region			Urban Water Supply	Agriculture		Total	Industry (%)	Urban Supply (%)	All Agriculture (%)
		Industry		Irrigation	Others				
I	Northeastern	9.90	2.66	33.13	4.14	49.83	19.9	5.3	74.8
II	Hai He-Luan He basin	6.82	3.62	27.47	3.35	41.26	16.5	8.8	74.7
III	Huai He basin	6.08	2.29	39.86	8.68	56.90	10.7	4.0	85.3
IV	Huang He basin	4.86	2.07	29.88	3.37	40.18	12.1	5.2	82.8
	II+III+IV	17.76	7.98	97.21	15.40	138.34	12.8	5.8	81.4
V	Yangtze River basin	40.92	7.23	101.00	15.06	164.16	24.9	4.4	70.7
VI	Southern	13.88	4.22	48.00	6.56	72.66	19.1	5.8	75.1
VII	Southeastern	4.61	1.36	20.21	2.72	28.89	16.0	4.7	79.4
VIII	Southwestern	0.33	0.09	4.83	1.19	6.44	5.1	1.4	93.5
	V+VI+VII+VIII	59.74	12.90	174.04	25.53	272.15	12.1	5.2	82.8
IX	Interior basins	1.45	0.56	38.97	17.25	58.23	2.5	1.0	96.5
	National total	88.85	24.10	343.35	62.32	518.55	17.1	4.6	78.2

SOURCE: Feilig, 1999.

Two competing factors will affect China's future demand: (1) growing water demand in the urban and industrial sectors due to further economic development and rapid urbanization; and (2) implementation of programs for efficient water use and conservation measures, particularly in the irrigation sector but also in all other sectors. Without sufficient progress in water use efficiency, Brown and Halweil (1998) projected that water demand in 2030 may reach 1,068 billion tons, nearly twice the consumption in 1998, given that by 2030 there will not be 1.2 billion poor Chinese, but 1.5 billion rather affluent Chinese. Between 2000 and 2010, China's population is projected to grow by 126 million, and a World Bank paper (2000b) estimates that China's water needs will increase to 670 billion m^3 by 2010. Only one-half of this incremental demand can be met through additional development of water resources, while the remainder will need to be met through water savings, or "deficit irrigation."

World Bank (2001b) estimates the demand for water in the 3-H basins in 2000 at 169 billion m^3, exceeding the supply by more than 30 billion m^3. In normal years, the irrigated and urban areas nationwide report an annual shortage of 30–35 billion m^3 and 5–6 billion m^3, respectively (World Bank various estimates). Yang and Zehnder (2001) project that even if improvements in irrigation efficiency reduces water demand in agriculture, the increase in water demand in the municipal and industrial sectors (6.5 billion m^3) far exceeds such decline, and an additional 4 billion m^3 of water will be needed within the coming decade in Beijing, Tianjin, and the three 3-H basin provinces.

As water use increases, particularly in industrial and urban sectors, wastewater discharges are also rapidly rising (about 42 billion m^3 from the urban and industrial sectors according to the Statistical Agency of the PRC, 2000 and 2001). The most ubiquitous pollutant is readily degradable organic material from domestic and industrial sources (World Bank, 2001b). China generates the largest total emissions of organic water pollutants in the world—the equivalent to the emissions of the United States, Japan, and India combined, as shown in Table 5.4 (World Bank, 2000b). The three major sources of water pollution are industrial, municipal, and agricultural (including fertilizer, pesticide, and livestock production) wastewater discharges.

The total volume of industrial wastewater discharge declined over the 1990s, particularly after 1995, when the government enacted a series of emergency measures, including the closing of 15 types of small-scale township and village enterprises throughout the country. Industrial wastewater treatment ratios (i.e., the proportion of total wastewater that passes through a treatment plant) have increased over the 1990s, from about 20 percent early in the decade through 77 percent in 1995 to 95 percent in 2000 (Statistical Agency of the PRC, 2000 and 2001). However, wastewater treatment effectiveness (i.e., the proportion of treated wastewater meeting relevant national standards) declined, and the World Bank (2001c) claims that this observation supports the view that the regulatory system provides good incentives for installing treatment facilities, but far less incentive to operate them since pollution levies are set too low.

Total wastewater flows and loads from municipal sources (22.1 billion m^3) now exceed those from industrial sources (19.4 billion m^3) (Statistical Agency of the PRC, 2000 and 2001). Double-digit growth of municipal wastewater treatment significantly improved the wastewater treatment ratio from 4 percent in 1991 to 10 percent in 1998 (World Bank, 2001c), but nonetheless Chinese cities still need massive investment just to maintain the current wastewater treatment ratio. World Bank (2001c) estimates that installed treatment capacity has to increase by six- or seven-fold to double the service level over the next 20 years.

Table 5.4

**Emissions of Organic Water Pollutants from Industrial Activities
(kilograms per day)**

Rank	Country	Total Emission		Emission Per Worker	
		1980	1993	1980	1993
1	China	3,358,203	5,339,072	0.14	0.15
2	United States	2,742,993	2,477,830	0.14	0.15
3	Japan	1,456,016	1,548,021	0.14	0.14
4	India	1,457,474	1,441,293	0.21	0.20
World total			18,745,247		

SOURCE: World Bank, 2000b.

Agriculture generates water pollution through nutrient runoff, pesticides, and emissions from intensive livestock production. It is especially noteworthy that World Bank (2001c) estimates the ratio of the chemical oxygen demand (COD) load because of untreated piggery wastes to total COD loads will increase from 28 percent in 1996 to 90 percent in 2010 in the central south, south, and east regions.

IDENTIFYING THE CONSEQUENCES OF FLOOD, WATER SHORTAGE, AND POLLUTION ON THE ECONOMY

Effects on Agriculture

Changes in diet and urbanization are the major driving forces for the restructuring of China's agriculture. Food preferences in China have rapidly changed to a more diverse diet—not only are Chinese eating more meat, but they are also increasing their consumption of vegetables, fruit, alcohol, sugar, eggs, and dairy products. Feilig (1999) points out that diet changes have affected agriculture in two ways: (1) conversion of land usage from grain production to production for vegetables, tobacco, orchards, or fish ponds; and (2) a massive expansion of feed grain cultivation to meet the increase in meat consumption. Because of the low energy efficiency of cycling grain through animals, more cropland is needed to support a meat-based diet than one based on grain.

Arable land is a precious resource for China's agriculture since most of the country is covered by mountains and deserts. For many years, the area of China's cropland was severely underestimated because it was based on the official estimates of about 95 million hectares from the Statistical Agency of the PRC. However, Feilig (1999) and World Bank (1997b) estimate the true area of China's cropland in the mid-1990s in the range of 132–136 million ha, and hence, grain yields per ha were overestimated and there is more room to increase productivity. According to the agro-ecological-zones model calculation (Feilig, 1999), potentially arable land for grain cultivation in China is estimated to be some 162 million ha and has the potential to produce 650 million tons of grain; so Feilig (1999) and World Bank (1997b) claim that the bottleneck for food production is not land, but the availability of investment capital, agricultural know-how, infrastructure in remote areas, and most importantly water.

China's water problems critically affect food production through droughts, flooding, and pollution (Feilig, 1999). Table 5.5 shows the areas affected by natural disasters out of about 130 million ha of the total farmland.

1. *Water shortage/droughts in North China:* In the north and northwest, China's agriculture suffers from severe and increasing water shortages, especially in downstream areas. For instance, droughts in 1999 caused damage of 89.4 billion yuan (US$ 10.7 billion or 1.1 percent of China's 1999 GDP) (*China Daily,* 2000). This water shortage is exacerbated by inefficient irrigation systems in upstream areas, increasing water consumption in urban areas, and possibly declines in precipitation. Water deficit is not only a volume problem, but more often a timing problem, since during the dry season, the rivers dry up for several months. Building more reservoirs and dams could reduce this problem.

2. *Flooding:* A complex system of lakes and wetlands serves as a natural defense against flooding, supplemented by man-made reservoirs and dikes. However, this system has been weakened by unplanned land uses over the past four decades—especially excessive logging, cultivation, construction, and industrial development. As a result, increased silt, industrial waste, and other solids flowed into the rivers and wetlands, raising water levels and reducing the capacity of lakes and reservoirs. *China Daily* (2001d) reports that among 85,000 reservoirs in China, over 30,000 are in dangerously poor condition. A massive deluge of the Yangtze River in 1998 killed 4,000 people and caused US$ 30 billion (255 billion yuan) in damage.

Table 5.5

Areas in China Affected by Natural Disasters, 1978–1997

Year	Total (million ha)	Drought (million ha)	%	Flood (million ha)	%	Other (million ha)	%
1978	21.8	18.0	82.4	0.9	4.2	2.9	13.3
1988	23.9	15.3	63.9	6.1	25.6	2.5	10.5
1996	21.2	6.2	29.4	10.9	51.1	4.1	19.5
1997	30.3	20.3	66.8	5.8	19.3	4.2	13.9

SOURCES: Feilig, 1999; primary source: SSB, 1997.

3. *Water pollution from industrial and urban areas:* This type of pollution includes oil products, heavy metals, phenol compounds, cyanide, arsenic, chlorinated hydrocarbons, sulfates, and nitrates that pose a major risk for agriculture. World Bank (1997d) estimates that increasing wastewater treatment from 30 to 50 percent would increase grain production by about 24 million tons by 2020. Pollutants, especially heavy metals, can accumulate in irrigated fields and enter the human food chain, thereby threatening public health as well. According to WRI et al. (1998), numerous studies have shown significant increases in cancer rates and deaths and birth defects in sewage-irrigated areas.

As shown in Table 5.5, water shortage is a serious and widespread problem. Irrigated grain yields are nearly double those of rain-fed grain, and nearly triple those of poorly endowed loess plateau (World Bank, 1992a). The 3-H basins produce one-half of the major grains in China, and their annual output value is over 120 billion yuan (US$ 14.5 billion) (World Bank, 2001d). Irrigation agriculture accounts for two-thirds of all production in the 3-H basins, but the shortage of irrigation water was estimated at about 32 billion m^3 in 1997 by the World Bank.

Floods affect mainly the southern areas and the lower reaches of rivers, which are the central core of Chinese agriculture, and the area prone to flood disaster (30 percent or more decreases in yields) accounts for 8 percent of China's sown area (Zhang, 1999). Flooding leads to fluctuation in grain production and thus threatens food supply stability for the Chinese population. Increased emergency buffer stocks for grain, improved food logistics, and a flexible import policy could reduce the impact of flood-related harvest fluctuation.

The Three Gorges Dam is intended to regulate China's Yangtze River and provide energy. While the government claims that large dams, such as the Three Gorges Dam, will end centuries of deadly floods and landslides, environmentalists warn that large dams tend to decrease the frequency of small floods but increase the likelihood of big ones. For example, if the 27.5 billion m^3 of water to be contained by the Three Gorges Dam were ever unleashed, an unprecedented catastrophe would occur (Kriner, 1999).

Effects on Industry, Municipal Water Supply, and Public Health

Most of China's impressive economic growth since 1978 has occurred in the industrial and commercial sectors, and as a result, industrial and urban demand for water increased over 500 percent since 1978, but actual water supplies have increased only around 100 percent. Out of 668 major cities, the central government classified 300 cities as short of water, 108 of which as having serious problems, and 60 as being critically short of water.

In general, water consumption by industry per unit of output value is more wasteful in China than in developed countries, but in Beijing, factories recycled 91.4 percent of all the water they used in 1996, a substantial increase from 58.2 percent in 1980; water withdrawal per 10,000 yuan output value was decreased from 155 m^3 in 1980 to 44 m^3 in 1996 (Lee, 1998). Average productivity of water use for Chinese industry is 24 yuan or $3 per m^3, but it is 67 yuan or $8 per m^3 in North China. World Bank (1997f) and a Chinese source (WRI et al., 1998) estimate the annual loss of industrial output due to water shortage in cities at 120 billion yuan or US$ 14.5 billion. However, these are overestimates since the marginal productivity is lower than the average productivity of water on which these estimates are based. Wang and Lall (1999) developed a production function using data from over 1,000 nationwide Chinese industrial plants in 1993, and they estimate the industrywide average output elasticity of water at 0.17 and the nationwide marginal productivity of industrial water use at 3.92 yuan/m^3 in 1993 prices, finding large variations across sectors and between regions, with the marginal value in the north being almost twice that of the south. World Bank (1997f) estimates the shadow price (i.e., marginal return) of water to industries in Shanxi province at 42 yuan/m^3 at the 1995 price level, using input-output analysis and the Linear Programming model. Water shortages also affect service industries in North China, and for instance, Beijing has been imposing strict water quotas on hotels, shops, government offices, and others (e.g., 100 liters of water per capita for public bathrooms, and 8 liters per car wash) since the beginning of 2002 (*China Daily*, 2001f). Water shortages in North China cities are already serious, estimated at approximately 5–6 billion m^3. Assuming the current marginal productivity of water in North China industries is 8–10 yuan/m^3 as a conservative estimate, we would calculate the lost industrial output to be annually well over 40–60 billion yuan. Without proper measures to mitigate this problem, economic losses in North China will rise as growing industrial and urban water demand increases both the volume of the water shortage and the marginal value of water.

Water shortages also affect municipal sectors. Household consumption in North China cities averages between 20 and 50 liters per capita per day (l/c/d), which barely exceeds the absolute minimum of 20 l/c/d for physiological and personal hygiene needs (World Bank, 1997d). Again, water pollution makes these public health problems worse. WRI et al. (1998) quote the estimate of Chinese sources that the impact of water pollution on human health is valued at about US$ 4 billion annually and claim that this is an underestimate. World Bank (1997d) also estimates the cost of water pollution in China at US$ 3.9 billion annually, using forgone wages as a conservative estimate of the essential value of human life. Even these conservative estimates amount to 1 percent of GDP as of 1995. While the majority of urban and some suburban residents now have access to tap water, more than one-half (53 percent) of the rural population does not. Only 6 of China's 27 largest cities meet the state standards for drinking water quality, and around 700 million people (half of China's population) drink water that fails to meet state standards (WRI et al., 1998).

China may need to increase its water supply capacity by 25 percent by 2010, an equivalent to building 600–800 new water treatment plants (each having a capacity of 400,000 m^3/day) (Silk and Black, 2000). Approximately US$ 700 million will be needed annually to meet projected municipal wastewater treatment demand in China in 2000 and beyond (*China Daily*, 2001f). According to *Xinhua* (2001a), Beijing plans to invest 17 billion yuan (US$ 2 billion) in the next five years to build 136 water saving projects in the industrial sector, to build 16 sewage treatment plants to ensure that 90 percent of sewage is treated, and to increase water prices from the current 2 yuan/m^3 to 6 yuan/m^3 in 2005. Since 1998, Shanghai has invested 1.4 billion yuan (US$ 169 million) to treat its rivers, especially Suzhou Creek, and the city's rivers have become noticeably clearer (*China Daily*, 2001a).

ALTERNATIVES TO ABATE THE PROBLEM, AND THE EXPECTED COST AND BENEFITS

Water Diversion from South to North

While medium-distance transfers from the Yellow River to large cities have been carried out as shorter-term projects, the Chinese government is about to start a massive water transfer from South to North as a longer-term strategic project. This project is composed of eastern, central, and western routes and is designed to divert water separately from the upper, middle, and lower reaches of the Yangtze River to meet the needs of North and Northwest China. The 500 billion yuan (US\$ 60 billion) project will divert 38–48 billion m^3 of water, 5 percent of the Yangtze annual flow (*China Daily*, 2001d).

Construction is planned to begin in 2002 on the 715-mile eastern route and 774-mile central route, and it is expected to be completed by 2010 at an approximate cost of 180 billion yuan (US\$ 22 billion), which will divert 16 billion m^3 or more (MacLeod, 2001). The western route, the most costly leg, still remains on the drawing board. World Bank (2000a) estimates the investment, operation, and maintenance cost roughly at 2 yuan/m^3 on average in 2000 prices.

The central government will share 60 percent of the total investment, and local authorities who will benefit from the project will pay the rest. To raise part of the investment, local governments will gradually increase present water-use charges, and the price for water will vary from region to region. The water price for residents in Beijing is expected to increase from 2 yuan in 2001 to 6 yuan per m^3 in 2005 (*China Daily*, 2001f). While irrigated farming can be quite profitable near large cities if high-valued fruits and vegetables are grown, average returns of irrigation water are as low as 2 yuan/m^3 (World Bank, 1997d). Raising prices is an incentive for people to conserve water, but some users, particularly farmers, may not be able to afford the water supplied by the project and instead will rely on pumping groundwater. Nevertheless, farmers will benefit indirectly since the shares for irrigation water from local sources will be preserved and there will be greater supplies of treated sewage water available for irrigation.

Beside construction cost, other costs such as for resettlement, the environment, and regional opportunity should be considered as well. About 370,000 people will be displaced in the transfer region along the eastern and central routes (*China Daily,* 2001h).

Brandon and Ramankutty (1993) note possibly serious environmental effects: (1) In the water exporting region there will be a reduction of flow in the Yangtze River, especially during the dry season, leading to possible seawater intrusion, with negative effects on delta fisheries and urban water supply in the Shanghai region. (2) In the transfer region, there will be a significant disturbance of aquatic ecology along the canals passing through major watersheds, secondary salinization of soil, and pollution of water by urban or industrial areas along the routes. However, Liu (1998) claims that most of the above adverse effects can be mitigated by proper technical measures (e.g., stopping water diversion when the flow to the lower Yangtze River falls below a critical level, lining the conveyance channel, and digging drainage canals), and that the south-north water transfer can instead yield environmental benefits, such as improving the channel of the lower Yellow River, enhancing the micro-climates of irrigated areas, ameliorating land subsidence and groundwater depletion, and replacing poisonously polluted water.

The opportunity cost of South China's regional development should also be considered. South China has more-abundant water resources than North China, but it also has a lot of industrial cities and irrigation fields. Therefore, although the marginal value of water resources is lower than in North China, water is not free in South China, and the amount of water available from South China is uncertain and limited. It is also doubtful that the Chinese government includes all of these nonconstruction costs into the project plans and budgets. Most of all, water supply from the project will be available only after 2010 and, therefore, cannot resolve imminent water shortages in the North China plain for the current decade.

Water Saving Technologies and Flood Control

Irrigation efficiencies vary depending on the irrigation technology used: 45 percent for earth canals, 70 percent for canal linings, 80 percent for low-pressure pipes, 85 percent for sprinklers, and 90 percent for micro-drip irrigation.

Considering that irrigation accounts for about 80 percent of China's total water use, a large-scale application of water-efficient irrigation technologies could save a huge amount of water. In Beijing, water saving irrigation technologies have been diffused since the mid-1980s and especially, sprinkler irrigation, which has reached over 30 percent of its total irrigated fields. Most of all, many farmers are willing to pay for the installation of water saving technologies to irrigate their fields. However, according to the concept of "real" water savings, which includes the return-flow factor (World Bank, 2000a), the net savings in the entire basin could be lower than expected because part of the water is lost upstream—because of old irrigation systems, returns by the hydrologic cycle, and through percolation and seepage—only then becoming available to downstream users (Yang and Zehnder 2001).

In the municipal sector, systems need to be set up to conserve water during distribution and consumption. Industrial development through restructuring improves water use efficiency and reduces water demand and pollution.

Flooding risk can be significantly reduced through modern flood mitigation technologies and reinforced levees. The *China Daily* (2001f) reports that since 1998, the central government has stepped up the development of water projects, with a total input of 136.4 billion yuan (US$ 16.4 billion)—reinforcing 30,000 kilometers of dikes and more than 450 reservoirs.

A Market Approach to Demand and Pollution Management

As water saving technologies mature, supply management becomes more expensive, and the costs are largely borne by nonbeneficiaries (Nickum and Easter, 1994). So far, government controls and water quotas have been the norm for demand management, especially in regulating industrial water demand. However, more-effective measures of demand management would be full-cost water pricing, which provides three substantial advantages: (1) providing water agencies with increased financial resources or enabling their privatization, (2) facilitating the reallocation of water to those with a greater willingness to pay (Nickum and Easter, 1994), and (3) reducing water demand and thereby postponing the need for investment, which releases financial resources for other activities and buys time for the development of improved technologies (Brandon and Ramankutty, 1993). In short, full-cost water pricing is a key link between supply and demand management—to finance urgent water supply projects and to defer less essential water demand.

Although many cities have increased water prices, the price of clean water is still low. While the marginal cost of new water projects is generally more than 1.20 yuan per m^3, the water tariffs range from 0.5 to 0.9 yuan per m^3 (World Bank, 1997f), discouraging wastewater reuse and the installation of water saving systems. Therefore, in the absence of water pricing reform, the success of other water saving measures is unlikely.

In the industrial sector, water pricing would be a more cost-effective way of water saving than regulatory methods such as water quotas. Pricing in urban areas may meet social resistance, and care must be taken to ensure the provision of the underprivileged with basic water and sanitation at affordable prices.

Pricing in rural areas will be difficult for cultural and technical reasons. Brown (2000) warns of the political risks of increasing water prices—the public response to raising water prices in China is akin to that of raising gasoline prices in the United States. However, beyond the cultural resistance, the increased water price may have detrimental effects on agriculture. Yang and Zehnder (2001) find that the share of irrigation costs in the total material cost (excluding labor) is about 10 percent for wheat and over 10 percent for corn in the North China plain provinces. By comparison, the proportion of irrigation cost is less than 2 percent in the United States, the European Union, Canada, and Australia. Therefore, it is claimed that increasing the price of irrigation water may further disadvantage grain farmers in North China and may reinforce the ongoing trend of substituting high-value cash crops for grain because of higher marginal returns to water from cash crops. In fact, in the past two years, Beijing has removed more than 10,000 ha of rice fields of the total 23,300 ha and plans to eliminate all rice from the fields by 2007 (*China Daily*, 2002).

A tradable water permit is another alternative for demand management. When water rights can be bought and sold, the market will naturally reallocate water to uses with higher economic value if transaction costs are low. In the long run, it also makes sense to concentrate water-intensive industries and urban development projects in the water-abundant south as people move from the agricultural to the industrial and service sectors.

Confronted with the concurrent needs to reduce pollution and increase industrial output and employment, the Chinese government has become interested in cost-effective pollution control. The current regulatory system provides a partial economic incentive to abate pollution by charging a levy on pollution only in excess of a given standard. Dasgupta et al. (2001) point out that the benefit of stricter effluent standards should be weighed carefully against the costs, and they conclude that changing to a full emissions charge system would greatly reduce abatement costs (for instance, at a 73 percent lower cost from their econometric case studies). Charges of between $3 and $30 per ton would be sufficient to induce 90 percent abatement of total suspended solid and other pollutants (Dasgupta et al., 2001).

Water Treatment and Recycling

Water recycling is a very cost-effective demand management approach, and moreover, wastewater reuse measures can tackle water pollution problems, too. Wastewater reuse can be applied to agriculture, industry, and municipalities.

The farmers in Beijing and Tianjin have used municipal wastewater for irrigation since the 1950s. Along with development of industries, the characteristics of municipal wastewater became more complicated and toxic. Because most wastewater was untreated and directly used for irrigation, it has seriously polluted soil, crops, and groundwater. To increase agricultural output and improve public health, municipal wastewater treatment should be strengthened and the quality of irrigation water should constantly be improved.

Industries can reuse wastewater inside factories after treatment or reuse treated municipal wastewater. Because industrial water uses are restricted by water use permit, wastewater reuse after treatment inside factories is highly developed. For the past 15 years, the industrial output in Beijing has increased by 650 percent, but total water withdrawal for industrial purpose has decreased by 57.5 percent. In 1996, the average recycling rate of industrial wastewater in Beijing was 91.4 percent, compared with about 40 percent for the national average and about 70 percent in OECD countries (SSB, 1997; World Bank, 1997d).

By 2000, 427 urban wastewater treatment plants had been built in China, and more than 300 are under construction. By 2005, China will double the daily capacity of wastewater treatment in cities throughout the nation, a great increase from 15 million m^3 in 2000 to 40 million m^3 in 2005. According to *China Daily* (2001a), Beijing's sewage treatment capacity reached 356.6 million tons in 2000, but only 18 million tons (less than 6 percent of the total) were recycled.

Lee (2000) claims the net present value of recycling projects is substantially higher than that of transfer projects. Moreover, the huge transfer project across the nation is associated with higher risk due to its size, its interdependencies among many regions, and its longer construction period. By contrast, the recycling project involves numerous small plant constructions; it has lower risk because each project is smaller in size and is independent from other regional projects and because the associated risks can be pooled among many plants. In addition, the transfer project involves a high risk of an irreversible environmental disaster, while the recycling project provides valuable environmental services, thereby contributing to public health and to increased productivity. Moreover, the water recycling project is more compatible with a market-based water resources management system (including full cost pricing and pollution charge) and should enhance municipalities' financial strength.

ECONOMIC AND SECURITY IMPLICATIONS

Effect of Water Problems on Productivity, Capital, and Labor

Our earlier sections estimate that the annual loss of unrealized industrial and agricultural potential due to water shortages already exceeds 100 billion yuan (more than 1 percent of the 2000 GDP), even without including labor loss due to public health damage. If effective policy measures are not taken, these water shortages and pollution will be magnified to the point of crisis in this decade and will seriously depress productivity growth, therefore reducing capital investment and increasing unemployment in North China. On the other hand, if proper measures are taken, water shortages could be a new growth opportunity.

To analyze the effects of water problems on the economy, this chapter focuses on the agricultural and industrial sectors. Once agricultural and urban users accept water as an economic commodity with a price, progress, including reallocation, will be possible. However, as Brown and Halweil (1998) maintain, unlike small countries such as Japan, Korea, and Taiwan, China is too big to simply divert irrigation water to urban and industrial water and to import most of its grain. Moreover, growth of agriculture and growth of industry are not mutually exclusive. Yao (1996) finds, using long-run regression data with national income indices of five sectors over 1952–1992, that agriculture has had a strong and positive effect on industrial growth and that simultaneous and mutually beneficial effects between agricultural and nonagricultural sectors (particularly township and village enterprises) have emerged since the economic reforms in 1979.

Water constraints in North China critically affect the total factor productivity of the agricultural sector. On the other hand, given the relatively high proportion of irrigation cost in grain production in North China, increasing the price of irrigation water is likely to reinforce the ongoing trend of shifts toward high-value cash crops. Average water use on irrigated land is about 4,500–6,000 m^3/ha, and the average yield of grain on this irrigated land is around 6,000 kg/ha in North China (roughly 1 kg grain to 1 m^3 water considering loss of water during transfer). Brown and Halweil (1998) and Yang and Zehnder (2001) point out that importing 20 million tons of grain per year from other provinces or the international market would free up 20 billion tons of water at a much lower cost than diverting water from the south, and this saved water could support urban and industrial water supply and the shift toward higher-value crops. Along with a trend toward an open economy, this transformation toward cash crops could increase productivity of China's agriculture if sufficient investment were made to help such transformation.

Along with water shortages, stricter pollution control is becoming an additional burden on industries, and this burden may reduce industrial productivity growth. However, as noted earlier, social costs of pollution treatment can be greatly reduced by a market approach. In fact, industrial pollution was disproportionately generated by a narrow section of the industry. By 1998, six industrial subsectors (pulp/ paper, food, chemicals, textiles, tanning, and mining) accounted for 87 percent of total industrial carbon dioxide load but only 27 percent of gross industrial output value. In particular, the pulp/paper sector accounted for nearly half of the carbon dioxide load while contributing only 2 percent of output value (World Bank, 2001c). Many enterprises in these sectors are small-scale and locally owned by county and township governments. Since they are important generators of local employment, it is difficult for local environmental protection bureaus to shut them down. However, since many of them are unprofitable, closing or consolidating them will improve both economic and environmental situations. The earlier section also mentioned that increasing wastewater treatment from 30 to 50 percent would increase grain production by about 24 million tons by 2020, an equivalent benefit from the south-north water transfer project. In sum, stricter pollution control probably has negative effects on employment, but not necessarily on industrial productivity growth, and it obviously has positive effects on agricultural productivity.

Agricultural employment is expected to fall from more than one-half of total employment in 1995 to one-quarter in 2020. Since a large majority of farmers' income still comes from farming, particularly in the interior provinces, scarce water resources in North China sharply limit agricultural income. Moreover, a substantial part of the migrant population and of the migration of farmers to urban centers is due to drought, desertification, and soil erosion and degradation (Economy, 1997). If irrigation water prices increase, many farmers are likely to quit producing grain, and emigration from rural areas will be accelerated. On the other hand, if agricultural restructuring from land-intensive grain production to labor-intensive cash crop production in the North China plain is successfully made, the expected agricultural unemployment would be eased.

Security: Food Sufficiency and Regional Conflicts

China experienced an unprecedented population increase from the 1950s to the early 1970s, creating a strong population momentum that is now driving China's population growth despite already low levels of fertility. Most projections assume that China's population will increase to some 1.48 billion by 2025. This causes a major problem for China's food supply: Within only three decades, the country will have to feed an additional 260 million people, a number roughly equivalent to the total population of the United States (Feilig, 1999). See Table 5.6.

By the end of 2000, China claimed to have about 500 million tons of grain in stock, enough to sustain consumption for a year. *China Daily* (2001e) reports the World Bank view that although China should increase its grain imports for the next 20 to 30 years, doing so would not present an undue financial burden within an importing range of 20–50 billion tons annually.

One major concern about reliance on increased grain import is "food security," but the strictly economic basis for this concern is dubious. Many Chinese policymakers consider that China needs to maintain a high level of self-sufficiency in grain (about 95 percent). However, Yang and Zehnder (2001) claim that it is wise for China to opt for increased grain imports, not only because the imports can alleviate water stress in North China, but because they also conform with the general idea of an open economy. Since China has limited land but an abundant population, it does not have a comparative advantage in land-intensive crops like grain, but it does have a comparative advantage in labor-intensive crops such as animal husbandry, horticulture, aquaculture, and processed agricultural products, making net trade surplus in agriculture from $57 million in 1980 to $6.8 billion in 1999 (Lin, 2000). Having joined the World Trade Organization (WTO), China will gain increased access to foreign agricultural product markets. If it can thereby increase its exports of labor-intensive agricultural products, the result will tremendously benefit rather than hamper Chinese agriculture in the long run (Lin, 2000).

Future Scenarios and Possible Adversities

If proper measures are taken, the water crisis in China can be avoided, or at least mitigated. The effects on economic growth of possible alternative scenarios are summarized in Table 5.7. During the 10th five-year plan (2001–2005), the Chinese government plans to invest over 400 billion yuan (US$ 48 billion) in water conservation projects (*China Daily*, 2001a), such as dike reinforcement and

Table 5.6

China's Food Demand, 1995–2020: Various Projections Compared
(millions of tons)

Year	Brown			Rosegrant et al.			Huang et al.			USDA			World Bank		
	P	D	I	P	D	I	P	D	I	P	D	I	P	D	I
1995	355	375	20	355	375	20	355	375	20	355	375	20	355	375	20
2000	342	405	63	385	403	18	410	450	40	362	387	25	411	420	9
2005	329	437	108	418	434	16	438	480	42	382	414	32	445	459	14
2010	317	472	155	453	468	15	469	513	44	403	443	40	483	502	19
2020	294	549	255	541	565	24	552	594	42	449	506	57	568	600	32

SOURCES: Feilig, 1999; primary source: OECD, 1997.
NOTES: P = production; D = demand; and I = imports.

shoring up reservoirs, and soil and water conservancy projects in the western region. If these moderate water conservation efforts are made as planned, a water crisis is unlikely to occur in the coming decade, and the base estimate of economic growth can be achieved. Moreover, under scenarios 2–4, if effective measures like full-cost pricing, water recycling, and pollution charges are successfully implemented (as assumed in scenarios 2–4), an even higher growth can be achieved. All these measures conform to market reform, decentralization, and an open economy.

Nonetheless, there still exists a possibility of serious economic adversities resulting from a water crisis. Construction of two routes of a gigantic south-north water transfer project started in 2002, and it is estimated to cost 180 billion yuan over the decade. But the real cost may escalate substantially, as was the case in the Three Gorges Dam project. Since the benefits of the transfer projects will not be realized until 2010, problems may arise if increased investment in the south-north water transfer substantially reduces investments in other water conservation projects. The adverse effects may be even worse than simply reducing water conservation efforts by one-half, since the costs of the transfer projects will displace other productive investments. Moreover, increasing the water price to collect the long-term construction costs will accelerate the collapse of grain production unless the investment in high-value-added agriculture is made. In this case, growth of total factor productivity (TFP), capital investment, and employment will decline, thereby seriously reducing sustainable economic growth of North China, which provides one-third of the national economy.

Moreover, Economy (1997) contends that while Beijing aggressively pursues plans for the river diversion, other provinces are resisting the project for political, economic, and environmental reasons and are, therefore, reluctant to contribute funds and manpower to the project. She warns, if these other provinces were forced to contribute, serious regional resistance and conflicts may develop. In other words, overenthusiasm of the central government may result in more serious economic problems if the large and expensive river diversion and water transfer projects are pursued in favor of the less dramatic but more efficient recycling and conservation efforts.

Table 5.7

Effects of Possible Alternatives and Scenarios on Economic Growth

Scenario	Factor Growth		Explanation
1 Base estimate (business as usual)—moderate water conservation efforts	TFP	1.0–1.5	Increased agricultural productivity as well as efficient resource allocation
	K	8.0–9.0	
	L	1.0–1.2	
2 Full-cost pricing with investment in high-value-added agriculture, reduction of grain production in north, and increase in grain imports	TFP	1.2–1.4	Increased agricultural productivity as well as efficient resource allocation
	K	8.5–9.5	Benefit from productivity increase, and relieved capital reserves from irrigation investment to more productive investment in industry and high-value-added agriculture
	L	1.2–1.7	Decreased grain-production labor offset by increased labor-intensive cash crop production
3 Increasing treatment capacities faster than wastewater increase, and reuse of municipal wastewater for irrigation	TFP	1.1–1.3	Increased agricultural productivity
	K	7.5–9.5	Mixed effects: displacement of other industrial investment, but more investment in irrigation facilities along with increased productivity
	L	1.2–1.7	Contingent on an increase in agricultural production
4 Shift from regulation to market-based pollution charge, leading to industrial restructuring	TFP	1.1–1.3	Efficient resource allocation among manufacturers and increased agricultural productivity
	K	8.5–9.5	Environmental goal achieved with less wastewater treatment costs, and more productive investment available from savings
	L	0.8–1.3	Unemployment from closing labor-intensive and pollutive small firms

Table 5.7—continued

Scenario	Factor Growth		Explanation
5 Full-cost pricing without invest-ment in high-value-added agri-culture	TFP	1.1–1.3	More efficient resource reallocation
	K	8.5–9.5	Benefit from productivity increase and better financing of public work
	L	0.0–0.5	Sharp decrease of labor in grain production
6 South-north transfer	TFP	1.0–1.2	No benefit until 2010
	K	7.5–8.5	Productive investments displaced by 180 million yuan investment over 10 years
	L	1.2–1.7	Employment growth due to this gigantic public works project
7 Water conservation efforts re-duced by one-half	TFP	0.5–0.6	Agricultural and industrial productivity growth seriously limited by the constraints of water shortage and pollution
	K	7.0–8.0	Under serious water constraints, capital investment also decreased although reduced water projects release other productive investments
	L	0.0–0.5	Unemployment from decreased (public) investment
8 Worst case: south-north transfer project displaces half of water conservation efforts, while in-creasing water prices	TFP	0.5–0.6	The same as reduced water projects case (scenario 7)
	K	6.5–7.5	Problems in reduced water projects case plus displacement of productive investment
	L	0.0–0.5	Decrease in other water projects offset by south-north transfer project, but higher water prices lead to decreased agricultural labors

NOTES: The base estimate of factor growth is from Wolf et al., 2000. K = capital growth. L = employment growth. The respective weights on employment growth and capital growth are 0.6 and 0.4.

Combining the most adverse scenarios in Table 5.7 (7 and 8), we estimate that China's economic growth would decrease by between 1.5 and 1.9 percent annually from the baseline annual growth of about 5 percent associated with the base case (scenario 1).

Table 5.7 summarizes the content and effects of eight scenarios (including the base case, scenario 1), which vary in their assumptions about China's adoption of the most efficient or least efficient policies and projects to relieve its serious water and pollution problems through the next decade.

Scenario 1 summarizes the base case drawn directly from prior RAND forecasts of China's macroeconomic growth through 2015.[2] Salient aspects of each scenario are summarized in the first column (Scenario) and final column (Explanation). The factor growth columns refer respectively to TFP, growth of capital (K), and employment growth (L). The estimates of these parameters in the base case (scenario 1) are drawn directly from the previously cited RAND work.

In scenarios 2 through 8, we describe circumstances in which China opts for differing, and successively less efficient, policies and projects for water pricing and pollution charges, wastewater treatment, water recycling, conservation, and south-north water transfers. If China opts for the more efficient policies, the risk of water and pollution crises would be substantially reduced, if not completely averted. That it might nevertheless choose less efficient ones, while not inevitable, is not implausible. Their plausibility might be traced to regional, provincial, bureaucratic, and political rather than economic considerations.

Indeed, recent statements from China's ministry of water resources indicate that the State Council has approved massive and costly transfer projects to channel water from the largest rivers in the south to northern cities like Beijing and Tianjin.[3]

---

[2]See Wolf et al., 2000, Table B.1, pp. 88–89, and Table 7, p. 36.

[3]See WSJ, November 27, 2002.

The parameter reestimates for each scenario (diverging from the base case) are based on the authors' judgments about how and how much the parameters for productivity, capital growth, and employment growth would be affected in the successive scenarios. For example, in the worst case—scenario 8—total factor productivity growth would decrease by between 0.5 and 0.9 percent annually (from an annual rate of 1.0 to 0.5 percent, or from 1.5 to 0.6 percent), growth of the capital stock would decrease by 1.5 percent annually (from 8.0 to 6.5 percent, or from 9.0 to 7.5 percent), and annual employment growth would decline by approximately 0.7 percent (from about 1.2 to 0.5 percent annually). Assuming that the factor shares are 60 percent for the labor income and 40 percent for the capital—which were used in RAND's prior work on China's economy[4]—would reduce the estimate of China's annual GDP growth by an upper-bound estimate of 1.9 percent. For scenario 7—also an adverse case—similar calculations yield a lower-bound estimate of forgone economic growth of 1.5 percent.

_____

[4]Wolf et al., 2000, Table B.1, p. 88.

Chapter Six

GDP EFFECTS OF AN ENERGY PRICE SHOCK

This chapter attempts to derive rough estimates of the adverse effects on Chinese GDP growth attendant upon an energy price "shock," defined as a substantial increase in oil prices, with ensuing empirical effects on such oil substitutes as coal and natural gas as outlined below. We begin with the case of a "severe" production cut and price increase and, for sensitivity purposes, also consider proportionately smaller "large" and "moderate" cases as well. As an ancillary effect in the context of China, such increases in the price of oil can be envisioned to produce an additional adverse impact on public health because of a renewed intensive use of "dirty" (high-sulfur) coal for electric power generation, industrial processes, space heating, and other purposes; however, the available literature does not offer a uniform estimate of that effect in terms of mortality and morbidity, in that the effects are difficult to separate from those of dust from construction sites and agricultural areas.[1]

We begin with the presentation of some basic data and projections on the Chinese energy sector, followed by a discussion of the effects of a severe increase in international oil prices. GDP effects are derived, and the three sensitivity cases are discussed.

---

[1]See, e.g., World Bank, 2001c, especially pp. 77–98.

SOME BASIC DATA ON THE CHINESE ENERGY SECTOR AND CHINESE GDP

Table 6.1 presents basic data and projections on Chinese primary energy consumption, while Table 6.2 presents analogous data for production.

Table 6.3 presents data and projections on Chinese GDP.

Table 6.4 presents data and projections on primary energy consumption (in Btu) per dollar of GDP for China and for the United States, as a crude measure of the energy intensity pattern of GDP. These data are rough estimates, particularly for the years after 2000, but provide a glimpse at the potential for reduced energy intensity of GDP available to the Chinese economy over time. Under an assumption that U.S. energy use is economically efficient as a first approximation, because it is driven largely (but certainly not wholly) by market forces, the difference between the energy intensities of Chinese and U.S. GDP may provide a very crude estimate of the future behav-

Table 6.1

Primary Energy Consumption in China
(quadrillion Btu)

Year	Coal	Natural Gas	Petroleum	Total
1980	12.5	0.6	3.8	17.3
1985	16.9	0.5	4.0	22.2
1990	20.7	0.6	4.9	27.0
1995	27.5	0.7	7.2	35.2
2000	22.7	1.2	9.7	36.7
2005	26.4	2.2	11.2	43.2
2010	33.3	3.4	14.2	55.3
2015	40.1	5.3	17.9	69.1

SOURCE: Energy Information Administration (EIA), *International Energy Database*, Washington, D.C., 2002.

NOTES: Totals may not sum because of other fuels and rounding. Figures for 2005–2015 are EIA projections, reference case.

Table 6.2

Primary Energy Production in China
(quadrillion Btu)

Year	Coal	Natural Gas	Petroleum	Total
1980	12.6	0.6	4.5	18.1
1985	17.7	0.5	5.4	24.3
1990	21.9	0.6	6.0	29.4
1995	28.3	0.7	6.4	35.4
2000	18.4e	1.1e	7.0	27.8e
2005	n.a.	n.a.	6.7	n.a.
2010	n.a.	n.a.	6.6	n.a.
2015	n.a.	n.a.	6.5	n.a.

SOURCE: EIA, *International Energy Database*, Washington,
D.C., 2002.

NOTES: Totals may not sum because of other fuels and
rounding. Petroleum includes crude oil, natural gas liquids,
and refinery processing gain. Figures for 2005–2015 are EIA
projections, reference case. Total is primary energy only.

e = estimated.

n.a. = not available.

ior of a Chinese economy driven increasingly by market forces and
confronted with a large increase in energy prices.[2]

OIL PRICE EFFECTS OF A "SEVERE" OIL SUPPLY
DISRUPTION

The most obvious "crisis" scenario in the energy context is a supply
disruption in international supplies of crude oil, perhaps attendant
upon a war in the Middle East affecting supplies from the Persian

---

[2]This is a very rough first approximation, since the economic structures of the Chinese
and U.S. economies, enjoying different comparative advantages in the world
economy, do and will continue to differ, even apart from differences in resource allocation outcomes yielded by government policies. These sorts of structural variations
yield differences in the relative sizes of the industrial, commercial, and residential sectors, and in the specific characteristics of each. Accordingly, there is no efficiency reason for the energy intensities of different economies in the aggregate to converge, but
the "starting points" of the Chinese and U.S. economies (say, in 1980) provide strong
grounds for the hypothesis that the energy intensity of the former will tend to move
toward that of the latter as market forces increasingly drive resource allocation.

Table 6.3

Chinese GDP
(billions of 2000 dollars)

Year	IMF	EIA	Wolf et al.
1980	169.8	n.a.	n.a.
1985	282.3	n.a.	n.a.
1990	412.2	448.3	n.a.
1995	726.6	n.a.	943.9
2000	1080.4	1168.2	1250.9
2005	n.a.	1669.4	1589.0
2010	n.a.	2389.6	2009.1
2015	n.a.	3284.2	2601.3

SOURCES: International Monetary Fund (IMF), *International Financial Statistics Yearbook 2001*, Washington, D.C., 2001; EIA, *International Energy Outlook 2001*, Washington, D.C., 2001, Appendix A; Wolf et al., 2000.

NOTES: IMF dollars were converted at the market exchange rate; EIA the reference case, and Wolf et al. the stable growth scenario. We converted to year 2000 dollars from Council of Economic Advisers, *Economic Indicators*, Washington, D.C., February 2002.

n.a. = not available.

Gulf, yielding a large increase in the world market price of oil and oil substitutes. Table 6.5 presents data on world production of petroleum.

There are some reasons to believe that the forecast of an increasing share of Persian Gulf output as a proportion of world output is somewhat unrealistic, although certainly plausible;[3] but since this study examines the effects of adverse circumstances, it is a useful general assumption. Let us adopt a worse-case assumption of an oil supply disruption in 2005, perhaps as a result of a major military

---

[3]See, e.g., Eliyahu Kanovsky, *The Economy of Saudi Arabia: Troubled Present, Grim Future*, Washington Institute for Near East Policy, Washington, D.C., September 1994.

Table 6.4

Primary Energy Consumption Per
Dollar of GDP
(in Btus)

Year	China	United States	China/U.S. (Btu ratio)
1980	76549	14945	5.1
1985	61006	12550	4.9
1990	46067	11727	3.9
1995	37292	11257	3.3
2000	26861	9956	2.7
2005	27187	9121	3.0
2010	27525	8415	3.3
2015	26564	7705	3.4

SOURCES: Tables 6.1 and 6.3; 10 percent
annual growth rate for 1980 through 1990
applied to Wolf et al., 2000, GDP projec-
tions. U.S. energy consumption is from EIA,
International Energy Database, 2002, and
International Energy Outlook 2001, 2001,
Washington, D.C. U.S. GDP is from Council
of Economic Advisers, *Annual Report of the
Council of Economic Advisers,* February
2002, and *Economic Indicators,* February
2002, Washington, D.C.; and from Office of
Management and Budget, *Budget of the
United States Government,* Washington,
D.C., fiscal year 2003.

conflict in the Middle East, which removes Persian Gulf oil from the
world market for, say, 10 years.[4] Let us assume in addition that the
world price elasticity of demand for oil is 0.10 (in absolute value) in
the short run, increasing by 0.025 each year for the duration of the
disruption.[5] The immediate effect upon the world market price of oil,
caused by a supply reduction of 28 percent (ignoring any immediate
production response outside the Persian Gulf), would be an in-

---

[4]This assumed magnitude and duration of the supply disruption are extreme, but they
serve to put a useful bound on the analysis of "crisis" effects on the Chinese economy.

[5]This assumption reflects the standard axiom that the elasticities of demand (in absolute value) and supply increase with time, that is, that greater adjustments to a shift in
exogenous conditions become economic as more time becomes available to make
them.

Table 6.5

World Petroleum Production and Consumption
(thousands of barrels per day)

Year	China	United States	Persian Gulf	World	Persian Gulf/ World Ratio	World Con- sumption
1980	2114	10809	18860	64139	.294	63067
1985	2505	11192	15668	59249	.264	60091
1990	2774	9677	16529	66743	.248	65974
1995	2990	9400	18351	69868	.263	69878
2000	3249	9000	20503	75614	.271	76515
2005	3100	9000	23800	84800	.281	85100
2010	3070	8700	28500	94700	.301	95000
2015	3050	9000	34600	106600	.325	106900

SOURCE: EIA, *International Energy Database*, 2002, and *International Energy Outlook 2001*, 2001, Washington, D.C.
NOTE: Production includes crude oil, natural gas and other liquids, and refining gain.

crease of about 280 percent, or roughly a quadrupling. Let us assume also that producers outside the Persian Gulf increase output in response to the price increase, by, say, 1 million barrels per day per year beginning in the second year (2006); a response is partly caused by the price increase and partly helps to moderate the price increase.[6] Let us assume that half of that total effect moderates prices, so that the true "supply" response is 500,000 barrels per day per year. Table 6.6 summarizes these production and price effects as rough parameters.[7]

EFFECTS ON CHINESE GDP

Oil Market Effects

One rough method for estimating the GDP effects of the simulated pattern of oil price increases is presented in Table 6.7. These estimates use Chinese GDP energy intensity data as shown in Table 6.4,

---

[6]In other words, part of the response is a movement along the supply curve, and part is a shift of the non–Persian Gulf supply curve resulting from an increase in the expected rate of return resulting from the price increase.

[7]Note that the price of the benchmark crude oil (Arabian light) was $34 per barrel in 1982, which is about $55 per barrel in year 2000 dollars.

Table 6.6

Simulated Petroleum Production and Price Effects

Year	Disruption	Non–Persian Gulf Supply Response (millions of barrels per day)	Net Production Cut	Price Increase (percentage)	Price (year 2000 $ per barrel)
2004	0	0	0	0	25.00
2005	23.8	0	23.8	281	95.25
2006	24.7	0.5	24.2	223	80.75
2007	25.6	1.0	24.6	185	71.25
2008	26.5	1.5	25.0	158	64.50
2009	27.5	2.0	25.5	138	59.50
2010	28.5	2.5	26.0	122	55.50
2011	29.6	3.0	26.6	110	52.50
2012	30.8	3.5	27.3	100	50.00
2013	32.0	4.0	28.0	92	48.00
2014	33.3	4.5	28.8	85	46.25
2015	34.6	5.0	29.6	79	44.75

NOTE: We assume an initial price of $25 per barrel (in year 2000 dollars).

in combination with assumptions about the Chinese demand elasticity for oil, the cross-elasticities of demand among primary fuels, and the evolution of the energy intensity of GDP. Let us assume that the Chinese demand elasticity for petroleum (and for energy generally) is equal to the world demand elasticity noted above.[8] Let us assume further that the energy content of a barrel of oil is 5,879 thousand Btu (EIA, *International Energy Database*, Washington, D.C., 2002). Table 6.7 shows estimates of these effects on Chinese oil consumption.[9]

One very rough method with which to estimate the GDP impact of the increase in oil prices and the attendant reduction in oil con-

---

[8]This is unlikely to be strictly correct; moreover, across nations the relative demand elasticities among alternative fuels are unlikely to be equal. But this assumption simplifies the analysis greatly, allows us to avoid the need for data that are unavailable in any event, and provides an answer unlikely to vary too greatly from the underlying truth. We also assume that Chinese energy demands do not affect world prices, a premise that is very likely to be correct except in some possible cases of such localized markets as (future) natural gas trade with Russia.

[9]We use the standard simple elasticity definition: percentage change in quantity equals elasticity times percentage change in price. For example, for 2005, 28.1 = 0.1 × 281.

Table 6.7

Chinese Oil Consumption Response to Price Increases

Year	Base Consumption	Reduced Consumption	Reduced Consumption (quadrillion Btus per year)
	(millions of barrels per day)		
2005	5.2	1.5	3.2
2006	5.5	1.5	3.3
2007	5.7	1.6	3.4
2008	6.0	1.7	3.6
2009	6.3	1.7	3.7
2010	6.6	1.8	3.9
2011	6.9	1.9	4.1
2012	7.3	2.0	4.3
2013	7.6	2.1	4.5
2014	7.8	2.2	4.6
2015	8.4	2.3	5.0

SOURCES: Table 6.1 (with interpolations), Table 6.6, and author computations.

sumption is to apply the estimated reduction in oil consumption (Table 6.7) to total primary energy consumption in China (Table 6.1) and the energy intensity of Chinese GDP (Table 6.4). This is a reasonable approach for purposes of rough estimation, in that the energy-using (or substitute) capital stock is fixed in the short run (by definition), so that lost output occasioned by the increase in the price of oil is driven by the price elasticity of demand for oil and the oil-intensity of GDP. Table 6.8 presents that simulation as an "energy inefficiency" scenario.

Note that the energy intensity of Chinese GDP predicted by the EIA, as shown in Tables 6.4 and 6.8, is roughly constant after 2005; it declines sharply between 1980 and 2000. It is reasonable to assume that a sharp increase in energy prices beginning in 2005 would induce a substitution toward more energy-efficient capital, among other important effects, so that the assumed Btu/GDP ratios in Table 6.8 may be unrealistic in terms of the conceptual experiment under examination here. Accordingly, let us assume that Chinese energy consumption per dollar of GDP declines between 2005 and 2015 at a rate of 1 percent per year, as opposed to the rate of less than about 0.2 percent per year in the inefficiency scenario. With a capital stock improving in terms of reduced energy intensity over the period, each unit of energy consumed would have a higher marginal value at the

Table 6.8

Simple Oil Consumption Effects on Chinese GDP, "Energy Inefficiency" Scenario

Year	Reduced Consumption (quadrillion Btu)	Btu/Dollar of GDP	Implied GDP Reduction (billions of 2000 $)	Base GDP (billions of 2000 $)	% Reduction
2005	3.2	27187	117.7	1589.0	7.4
2006	3.3	27254	117.4	1665.3	7.1
2007	3.4	27322	124.4	1745.2	7.1
2008	3.6	27389	131.4	1829.0	7.2
2009	3.7	27457	131.1	1916.8	6.8
2010	3.9	27525	141.7	2009.1	7.1
2011	4.1	27330	150.0	2115.6	7.1
2012	4.3	27136	158.5	2227.7	7.1
2013	4.5	26944	167.0	2345.8	7.1
2014	4.6	26753	175.7	2470.1	7.1
2015	5.0	26564	184.5	2601.3	7.1

SOURCES: Tables 6.3 and 6.4 (interpolated), Table 6.7, and author computations.

higher prices and improved energy efficiency. So let us assume that the demand elasticity (in absolute value) increases only from 0.1 to 0.2 over the period.[10] Table 6.9 outlines this scenario.

Oil Import Cost. An increase in the amount of real resources that China would have to send (pay) overseas in the face of a rise in international oil prices represents a loss of national wealth relevant to the reduction in GDP under examination here. Table 6.10 presents calculations of the increase in the Chinese oil import cost attendant upon the oil supply disruption hypothesized above. We assume a reduction in oil consumption at the average of those shown in Tables 6.8 and 6.9; and we assume, for "severe-case" analytic purposes, constant Chinese oil output at 3,100 thousand barrels per day, as shown in Table 6.5. This loss of national wealth would be likely to have an additional effect on energy consumption, which must be a normal good in the economic sense,[11] but that effect is ignored here, as is the adverse exchange rate effect of increased spending on imported oil.

---

[10]In the former case, the demand elasticity rises from 0.1 in 2005 to 0.35 in 2015.

[11]A normal good is one for which demand rises as income (or wealth) rises.

Table 6.9

Simple Oil Consumption Effects on Chinese GDP, "Energy Efficiency" Scenario

Year	Reduced Consumption (quadrillion Btu)	Btu/Dollar of GDP	Implied GDP Reduction (billions of 2000 $)	Base GDP (billions of 2000 $)	% Reduction
2005	3.2	27187	117.7	1589.0	7.4
2006	2.9	26915	107.7	1665.3	6.5
2007	2.7	26646	101.3	1745.2	5.8
2008	2.7	26380	102.4	1829.0	5.6
2009	2.6	26116	99.6	1916.8	5.2
2010	2.6	25855	100.6	2009.1	5.0
2011	2.6	25596	101.6	2115.6	4.8
2012	2.7	25340	106.6	2227.7	4.8
2013	2.7	25087	107.6	2345.8	4.6
2014	2.7	24836	108.7	2470.1	4.4
2015	2.8	24587	113.9	2601.3	4.4

SOURCES: Tables 6.3 and 6.4 (interpolated), Table 6.7, and author computations.

Table 6.10

Increase in Chinese Oil Import Cost

Year	Base Imports	Disruption Imports	Base Import Cost	Disruption Cost	Difference	% of Base GDP
2005	2.1	0.6	19.2	20.9	1.7	0.1
2006	2.4	1.0	21.9	29.5	7.6	0.5
2007	2.6	1.1	23.7	28.6	4.9	0.3
2008	2.9	1.4	26.5	33.0	6.5	0.4
2009	3.2	1.8	29.2	39.1	9.9	0.5
2010	3.5	2.0	31.9	40.5	8.6	0.4
2011	3.8	2.3	34.7	44.1	9.4	0.4
2012	4.2	2.6	38.3	47.5	9.2	0.4
2013	4.5	2.8	41.1	49.1	8.0	0.3
2014	4.7	3.0	42.9	50.6	7.7	0.3
2015	5.3	3.5	48.4	57.2	8.8	0.3

SOURCES: Tables 6.1, 6.2, 6.7, 6.8, 6.9; author computations.

NOTES: We assume $25 per barrel price in absence of supply disruption. Imports are in millions of barrels per day. Costs are in billions of year 2000 dollars.

Fuel Substitution Effects. The adverse GDP effects summarized in Tables 6.8 and 6.9 are driven by the effect of a reduction in the consumption of oil in terms of the energy intensity of GDP. Some of that adverse effect would be offset by substitution of other primary fuels—coal and gas—for oil. Rothman et al.[12] estimate a cross-elasticity of demand among fuels of 0.33 for 53 nations, an estimate very likely to represent a long-run estimated parameter; for China under the conditions postulated here, a much smaller short-run cross-elasticity of demand is reasonable. Bjoner and Jensen have estimated more recently for Danish industry a cross-elasticity of demand range of 0.05–0.57.[13] For China, we assume heavy constraints on increased coal use due to environmental/health concerns, and on increased gas use because of importation costs and constraints. Accordingly, we assume a cross-elasticity of fuels demand of 0.02 for China. Table 6.11 summarizes the fuel substitution effect for Chinese GDP; we ignore price effects for coal and natural gas, and we assume the average energy intensity of GDP from Tables 6.8 and 6.9.

Table 6.11

Fuel Substitution Toward Coal and Gas

Year	Base Consumption		Disruption Consumption		Total Btu Increase	Btu/GDP (ratio)	Increased GDP	% Increase
	Coal	Gas	Coal	Gas				
2005	26.4	2.2	27.9	2.3	1.6	27187	58.9	3.7
2006	27.7	2.4	28.9	2.5	1.3	27085	48.0	2.9
2007	29.0	2.6	30.1	2.7	1.2	26984	44.5	2.6
2008	30.3	2.9	31.3	3.0	1.1	26885	40.9	2.2
2009	31.8	3.1	32.7	3.2	1.0	26787	37.3	1.9
2010	33.3	3.4	34.1	3.5	0.9	26690	33.7	1.7
2011	34.6	3.7	35.4	3.8	0.9	26463	34.0	1.6
2012	35.9	4.1	36.6	4.2	0.8	26238	30.5	1.4
2013	37.2	4.4	37.9	4.5	0.8	26016	30.8	1.3
2014	38.6	4.8	39.3	4.9	0.8	25810	31.0	1.3
2015	40.1	5.3	40.7	5.4	0.7	25576	27.4	1.1

NOTE: Consumption is in quadrillion Btu. GDP is in billions of year 2000 dollars.

---

[12]Dale Rothman, J. Hong, and T. Mount, "Estimating Consumer Energy Demand Using International Data: Theoretical and Policy Implications," *Energy Journal*, Vol. 15, No. 2, 1994, pp. 67–88.

[13]Thomas Bue Bjoner and Henrik Holm Jensen, "Interfuel Substitution Within Industrial Companies—An Analysis Based on Panel Data at Company Level," *Energy Journal*, Vol. 23, No. 2, 2002, pp. 27–50.

Table 6.12 aggregates the separate effects on Chinese GDP for the "severe" disruption case assuming the "energy efficiency" scenario from Table 6.9, in percentage change from the baseline in Table 6.3. As a crude summary, an increase in the price of oil following a "severe" cutoff of Persian Gulf exports would reduce annual Chinese GDP by about 3.5–4.0 percent over the period 2005–2015.

Effects of Smaller Disruptions. For purposes of sensitivity analysis, we consider significant but smaller disruptions in the supply of oil: A "large" disruption might be defined as two-thirds of the "severe" case, while a "moderate" disruption might be defined as one-third of the "severe" case. If we maintain our elasticity assumptions as outlined above,[14] the price, consumption, import, and fuel substitution effects remain proportional. Accordingly, a "large" disruption engendering effects at two-thirds of the "severe" case would reduce annual Chinese GDP by about 2.3–2.7 percent. A "moderate" disruption, one-third of the "severe" case, would reduce annual GDP by about 1.2–1.4 percent.

Table 6.12

**Summary of GDP Effects, "Severe" Disruption
(percentage)**

Year	Oil Consumption	Import Cost	Fuel Substitution	Total
2005	(7.4)	(0.1)	3.7	(3.8)
2006	(6.5)	(0.5)	2.9	(4.1)
2007	(5.8)	(0.3)	2.6	(3.5)
2008	(5.6)	(0.4)	2.2	(3.8)
2009	(5.2)	(0.5)	1.9	(3.8)
2010	(5.0)	(0.4)	1.7	(3.7)
2011	(4.8)	(0.4)	1.6	(3.6)
2012	(4.8)	(0.4)	1.4	(3.8)
2013	(4.6)	(0.3)	1.3	(3.6)
2014	(4.4)	(0.3)	1.3	(3.4)
2015	(4.4)	(0.3)	1.1	(3.6)

SOURCE: Tables 6.8–6.11.

NOTES: Oil consumption effect is the average of Tables 6.8 and 6.9. Numbers in parentheses are negative.

---

[14]This is reasonable, in that the assumed elasticities at any given price are more likely to hold for smaller price changes than for larger ones.

PART III

FINANCIAL FAULT LINES

Chapter Seven

CHINA'S FRAGILE FINANCIAL SYSTEM AND THE STATE-OWNED ENTERPRISES

This chapter seeks to identify the major problems in China's financial system that could escalate to a financial crisis and stifle economic growth in the next decade.[1] As will be shown below, the ailing state-owned enterprises (SOEs) lie at the center of China's financial problems. China's major banks themselves are SOEs. For these reasons, we discuss briefly the economic consequences of the lack of progress in enterprise reform, particularly its impact on the financial system.

China's financial system has undergone dramatic changes in the past two decades. Of particular interest are the changes in its organizational structure. By the year 2000, the mono-bank system of the pre-reform era had developed into a multilevel system with a central bank, 18 commercial banks, and a variety of financial institutions.[2] There are also rudimentary financial markets dealing in various financial instruments. A set of laws defining the specific functions of these institutions has been promulgated. In addition, the system is

---

[1]The discussion here is limited to the domestic aspects of the financial system.

[2]The People's Bank of China (PBC) is the central bank. The state banks include four state-owned commercial banks: the Bank of China (BOC), the Industrial and Commercial Bank of China (ICBC), the Construction Bank of China (CBC), and the Agricultural Bank of China (ABC). There are also three state-owned policy banks: the State Development Bank, the Agricultural Development Bank, and the Export-Import Bank. For brief information on the 11 nonstate banks, see Almanac, 2001, pp. 32–48. Other financial institutions include urban and rural credit cooperatives or banks, investment trusts, financial companies, insurance companies, brokerage houses, and stock exchanges. A number of foreign banks have branches in China.

no longer purely state owned (or collectively owned). It has become a mixed system, with at least one private bank and a number of branches of foreign banks. However, in sharp contrast to the notable accomplishments in organizational restructuring, little progress has been made in changing the functions of the financial institutions as specified by the laws and regulations. While the rest of the economy moves steadily toward a market-oriented system, the financial sector remains virtually unchanged. Consequently, the system now faces some deep-rooted problems.

AN INEFFECTUAL CENTRAL BANK

The first major weakness of the financial system is its ineffectual central bank. The PBC was first established as a central bank in 1983. But it was not until 1995 that the People's Congress enacted the PBC Law, which provided the legal framework for the role and functions of the PBC as China's central bank. The fundamental task of the PBC is to maintain monetary stability and financial health of the economy.[3] While the goal is clearly specified and the organizational structure is in place, the PBC lacks the autonomy to set monetary policies independently and the appropriate instruments to implement monetary policies.

The PBC Law stipulates that the PBC is to formulate and implement monetary policy "under the leadership of the State Council" (Dai and Gui, 1997, p. 275). Thus, by design, key policy decisions on annual money supply, interest rates, and the allocation of credit must be approved by the State Council.[4]

---

[3]By monetary stability, we mean economic growth with neither high inflation nor deflation.

[4]Apparently to justify the subordination of the PBC to the State Council, Liu Hongru, former Vice Governor of the PBC, argues that not all independent central banks can control inflation and that some less independent ones can (Hainan, 1992, p. 179). The implication is that central bank independence is neither a necessary nor a sufficient condition for inflation control. That being the case, the PBC's lack of independence should not be a serious handicap. Some economists in China disagree. They believe that central bank independence is of paramount importance (Dong, 1994, p. 970; DRC, 1994, p. 70). Empirical studies do provide some foundation for their view. For example, based on data for 16 countries in 1955–1990, Long and Summers have found a strong inverse correlation between central bank independence and inflation (Long

The lack of independence could have serious consequences if the primary goals of the government and the central bank come into conflict. The overriding goal of the government is economic growth, and that of the PBC, monetary stability. In principle, the two ends need not be competing. Indeed, the PBC Law stipulates that the aim of monetary policy is to maintain monetary stability and thereby promote economic growth. The former is to be the prerequisite for the latter. However, Zhou Zhengqing, the Vice Governor of PBC, has a different interpretation of the PBC Law. He lists price stability and economic growth as two separate, parallel goals (Hainan, 1992, p. 25). The subtle difference in perception is important, because it raises the question of which policy objective would take precedence should a conflict arise. The answer seems clear. The PBC is to operate under the direction of the State Council, which means that central bank policies must be subordinate to government policies.

Worse still, until 1998, branches of the central bank were set up at each administrative level. Thus, there were 31 branches at the provincial level and about 2,000 branches at the county level. Very often, officials of local governments pressured the local branches of the central bank to increase their loans, making it difficult for the PBC to control money supply. The local branches of the PBC had to accommodate the demands of the local officials, mainly because bank managers were controlled by local governments and party committees, and their careers depended on their relationship with the local officials.

The situation changed in 1998 when the government reorganized the PBC into nine regional branches. The intent was to remove the possibility of the local officials interfering with central bank policy. The new organizational structure represented a step toward independence of the PBC from local governments. How effective it will be remains to be seen, because the influence of local government officials is based not only on geographical proximity, but also on the network of their personal relationships.

Another factor limiting the effectiveness of central bank policy is that effective instruments of monetary policy available to the PBC are

---

and Summers, 1992, pp. 103–108). See also Alesina, 1988; Grilli, Masciandaro, and Tabellini, 1991; and Cukierman, 1992.

largely missing. In theory, a number of policy instruments are at its disposal, including both direct controls over the volume and distribution of bank credit and indirect measures such as changing the reserve requirements, setting interest rates, lending to commercial banks, and conducting open market operations. In practice, the indirect measures are of limited use, except perhaps lending to commercial banks. Consider, for example, open market operations. As noted by Cheng (1999, p. 14), in the late 1990s, the total outstanding stock of treasury bills was too small to accommodate open market operations without causing large swings in interest rates. In 1999, the PBC injected 192 billion yuan into the money supply through open market operations (Liu, Wang, and Li, 2001, p. 56). This amounted to only 12 percent of the increase in broad money supply in that year (SA 01, p. 79). Likewise, the volume of rediscounts is too small to be of any significance. Changing the rediscount rate would raise or lower the capital costs to the commercial banks and signal that the central bank is tightening or loosening credit. Indeed, since 1998, the PBC has adjusted the rediscount rate several times. However, the state banks are rather insensitive to changes in the rediscount rate, because, like all SOEs, they are not overly concerned with the cost of borrowing. The PBC can also set the basic interest rates for commercial bank lending and deposits, in order to influence money supply through the effect of interest changes on the demand for and supply of bank funds. But again, the PBC's interest rate policies are subject to various constraints. The government has a long established policy to set lending rates below market levels so as to subsidize the SOEs, and that leaves little room for the PBC to raise lending rates. Nor does it have much leeway in lowering these rates, because a lower lending rate would adversely affect the banks' profitability since there are lower bounds to the deposit rates.

As will be noted below, personal savings are the most important component of national savings and the bulk of personal savings is deposited in banks. If deposit rates are low, particularly relative to inflation, people might reduce their bank deposits, thus shrinking the supply of banks' loanable funds. In theory, raising the reserve ratio would force the banks to rely more heavily on central bank credit. However, because central bank lending is subject to government control, that too may not be an effective policy instrument. In the end, the PBC has to rely on direct controls to curb inflation. The problem with direct controls is that these measures are relatively inflexible, and in recent years their effectiveness has been eroded by financial transitions outside the formal sector.

To sum up, the institutional framework for central bank management is inherently flawed in that the PBC remains a tool of government policy, passively accommodating what the government dictates, rather than actively and independently controlling money supply to achieve monetary stability. Aside from being primarily a monetary policy implementer rather than a policymaker, the PBC is also poorly equipped to control money supply. Its attempts to carry out monetary policies have been persistently undermined by local governments, commercial banks, and other financial institutions. The weaknesses of the PBC are evidenced by the four episodes of rapid inflation during the two decades since 1978 (SY 00, p. 289; Hainan, 1992, pp. 29–34). In all cases, inflation was preceded by large and abrupt increases in money supply (Yi, 1994, pp. 50–51; SA 01, p. 79). Not surprisingly, an empirical study based on data for 1979–1993 by the State Statistical Bureau (SSB) finds a significant relationship between money supply and price changes, given a lag of two years: The elasticity of retail price changes with respect to changes in money supply was as high as 0.32 (Ren, Qiu, and Yan, 1995).

A FRAGILE COMMERCIAL BANKING SYSTEM

A second major weakness of China's financial system is its fragile banking sector. Table 7.1 shows the structure of assets of financial institutions in China in 2000.[5] Clearly, the banking sector is by far the majority component of the financial system. This sector's assets accounted for 96 percent of the total for the financial system as a whole. The banking sector, in turn, is dominated by four state banks. The predominance of the state banks means that whatever troubles the state banks will hurt the banking and even the entire financial

---

[5]The data for Table 7.1 are drawn from China's financial statistics yearbook. Possibly, statistics for some financial institutions have not been included, such as some provincial investment trusts and private credit unions. But the omissions are believed to be relatively small.

Table 7.1

Assets of China's Financial Institutions, 2000
(in billions of yuan)

Financial Institution	Total Assets
Banks	17,507.5
State-owned commercial banks	
Industrial and Commercial Bank of China	3,973.7
Bank of China	2,893.3
Construction Bank of China	2,531.7
Agricultural Bank of China	2,184.9
Policy banks	
State Development Bank	808.3
Agricultural Development Bank	770.8
Export-Import Bank	68.3
Others	
Bank of Communications	628.2
CITIC Industrial Bank	234.6
Regional banks	1,057.1
Urban credit cooperatives	678.5
Rural credit cooperatives	1,393.1
Foreign banks	285.0
Investment trusts	378.4
Security dealers	68.8
Insurance companies	124.1
Total	18,078.8

SOURCE: Almanac, 2001, pp. 362–363, 421–436, 474–489.

NOTES: The regional banks include the Merchant Bank, Guangdong Development Bank, Shanghai Pudong Development Bank, China Everbright Bank, Shengzhen Development Bank, Fujian Development Bank, Huaxia Bank, China Minsheng Bank, and Yantai Housing Savings Bank. The investment trusts include China International Trust and Investment Corporation (CITIC), Zhong Mei Trust and Investment Corporation, and Shanghai Investment Trust Corporation. The security dealers include the Huaxia Security Company and the China Southern Security Company. The insurance companies include nine life and property insurance companies.

system. It so happens that the state banks are facing some formidable problems at this stage. Nonperforming loans in their portfolios have been piling up, and their profits are dwindling.

The Chinese define bad loans to include overdue loans (yuqi daikuan), i.e., loans that have not been repaid by the due date; nonperforming loans (daizhi daikuan), i.e., loans that have been overdue for over two years; and nonrecoverable loans (daizhang daikuan), i.e., loans to be written off as losses. There is no definitive estimate of the size of bad loans that the state banks have accumulated. Available estimates vary widely. According to Dai Xianglong, Governor of China's central bank, bad loans of the four state banks amounted to only 9 percent of GDP, not alarmingly large, and roughly the same as that in Japan in 1997 (Zhao, 2001, p. 3; *The Economist*, March 8, 1997, p. S16). However, unofficial estimates are considerably higher, 23–33 percent of GDP in 1999 (Yuan, 2000, p. 12; SY 01, pp. 49, 638). Higher still are some estimates by researchers outside China, which put the share of bad loans at 40–53 percent of GDP in 1999 (Zhao, 2001, p. 3; WSJ, September 29, 1999, p. A14; SA 00, p. 14). The highest estimate is that by Standard and Poor's, which placed bad loans at 60 percent of GDP for 1997 (*The Economist*, February 14, 1998, p. 37).

Two tentative conclusions can be drawn from the various estimates. First, the problem of bad debts in the state banks is serious. Even by official measures, the size of bad loans is rather large, about 26.6 percent of total loans in 2000 (*Shihjie ribao* [Chinese Daily News], November 2, 2001, p. C6). In fact, the true size of the bad loans is, in all likelihood, considerably larger than the official figures suggest, because the banks often roll over the bad loans, so they do not show on their balance sheets (Yuan, 2000, p. 12; *Jingji ribao* [Economic Daily], February 20, 1995, p. 7). Moreover, the definition of bad loans used by Chinese banks is much more lenient than Western standards.[6]

Second, the problem is apparently worsening in recent years. According to one report, the bad loan ratio has been rising by 2 percentage points a year (*The Economist*, September 13, 1997, p. 26). Even if the ratio remained unchanged, the amount of bad loans in absolute terms has been rising rapidly, because total loans by state banks increased 1.9-fold during 1995–2000 (SY 96, p. 614; Almanac, 2001, p. 375).

The large bad debt overhang is merely a symptom of some deep-rooted problems in the banking sector: the persistence of government-directed policy loans; the perverse behavior of the state banks'

---

[6]Beginning in 2002, China adopted the international risk classification system, so that the official bad loan ratio may have risen (*Xin bao* [Hong Kong Economic Journal], May 25, 2002, p. 10). The implication is that recent ratios are on the low side by international standards. Thus, *The Economist* (March 8, 1997, p. S16) believed that the bad loan ratio may be twice the official estimate if a stricter standard is used.

major borrowers, the SOEs; and shortcomings in the management of the state banks themselves.[7] In sharp contrast to the policy of sustained economic liberalization of the real (nonfinancial) sector, the Communist Party leaders had, from the very beginning, decided to retain authoritarianism over the financial sector. Accordingly, the state banks are given dual functions. They serve, first of all, as financial agents to support various government policies, and secondarily, as financial intermediaries in a market economy that mobilize savings and allocate capital to screened borrowers based on credit and risk assessment and corporate governance. The Commercial Bank Law promulgated in 1994 states that, after a transition period of unspecified duration, all banks are to operate as independent legal entities responsible in management, risk taking, profit and loss, and general prudence. In the interim, however, they must lend according to the needs of the national economy, social developments, and the state's industrial policy as mandated by the State Council. Specifically, these policy loans include loans to finance infrastructure investment, fixed investment and working capital of the SOEs, sectoral or regional development assistance, and credit for procurement of key agricultural products and for mandatory imports. They also include loans to finance such programs as poverty alleviation in minority areas, education and housing, and most important, financial support of insolvent SOEs for fear that massive unemployment from bankrupt SOEs might cause widespread social unrest.

Not only the central government but also local governments actively interfere with bank lending. As noted earlier, government officials often pressure banks to support local expansion programs and pet projects. These projects are generally designed with little regard to the community's comparative advantages or economies of scale. Examples are the numerous small cigarette plants, wineries, coke and petroleum refineries, and textile factories. Local officials have enormous leverage over the banks, because they administratively supervise the local branches of the state banks, they negotiate with the central bank over the amount of loan quota the local banks can lend, they decide how much of the existing loans to the local SOEs are to be repaid, and they are in a position to assist the banks in such mat-

---

[7]Policy loans refer to loans made by the state banks at the instruction of the government, to support certain government policies, such as subsidizing ethnic groups.

ters as hiring, housing, and education of the bank employees' children.

The dual roles of the state banks, both as the government policy agents and as market-driven financial intermediaries, are obviously inconsistent. When conflicts occur, the latter function is sacrificed. For this reason, the process of transforming the state banks into genuine commercial banks has been thwarted for decades. In an attempt to resolve the conflict, the government set up three policy banks in 1994 to take over policy lending, so that the four state banks can henceforth concentrate on commercial lending according to market principles.[8] However, establishing policy banks helps but does not relieve the state banks of their existing heavy burden, because the policy banks only took over a small portion of the policy loans that the state banks accumulated.[9] The four state banks are still stuck with large chunks of outstanding policy loans. Worse still, they are not entirely free from new policy lending yet. By extending policy loans, the state banks are actually performing many fiscal functions of the government, which the state used to finance through the state budget. This was necessary because the state's fiscal capacity to mobilize resources through the state budget has diminished sharply.[10] Meanwhile, the demand for public services has been rising. Under the circumstances, the government simply shifts the fiscal burden to the state banks. Unless and until the state banks' burden is lifted, they have little choice but to continue their policy lending.

The problem with policy lending is that these loans are made mainly on the basis of social and political considerations, rather than on commercial criteria, such as financial viability of projects and creditworthiness of borrowers. The chance of their being repaid is minimal. The result is that most if not all of these loans become bad

---

[8]The three policy banks are the State Development Bank, the Export-Import Bank, and the Agricultural Development Bank. They took over the policy lending of the investment companies of the State Planning Commission, the Bank of China, and the Agricultural Bank of China, respectively.

[9]The Agricultural Bank of China and the Industrial and Commercial Bank of China have transferred some policy loans to the Agricultural Development Bank. But the State Development Bank has not inherited any policy loans from the Construction Bank of China (World Bank, 1996, p. 33).

[10]The amount of resources mobilized through the state budget declined from 31 percent of GDP in 1978 to 15 percent in 2000 (SA 01, p. 67).

loans. To be sure, some policy loans are based on economic considerations, e.g., loans to finance technical innovation and industrial restructuring. These loans are made on the assumption that government bureaucrats are farsighted enough to determine what will be viable and profitable industries in the future. More often than not, the officials err and the loans turn sour. Examples are the many duplicative plants built by local governments (Wu, 1992, p. 50).

Another major factor underlying the growth of bad loans is the poor performance of the SOEs, the most important borrowers of the state banks. To a large extent, the state banks' bad loans originate in their lending to the SOEs.[11] Why have so many loans to the SOEs turned bad? To begin with, the debt-to-equity ratio of the SOEs is rather high, about 79 percent in 1996. The relatively high ratio suggests that the SOEs have to carry a rather heavy debt burden. Debt service alone amounted to 10 percent of GDP in 1997 (Zhao, 2001, p. 25; SA 00, p. 14). The high debt-equity ratio should cause no problem if the SOEs were profitable. Unfortunately, this was not the case. Various indicators suggest that the profitability of the SOEs have been on the decline since 1978.[12] Worse still, not only do many SOEs fail to make profits, they have substantial operating losses. In 1997, over 39 percent of all the industrial SOEs incurred operating losses, compared to 19 percent in 1978. Their losses totaled 74.4 billion yuan in 1997, compared to 4.2 billion in 1978. In 1997, their losses actually exceeded earnings of the profitable industrial SOEs by a wide margin (Zhang, 1998, p. 33; SA 98, p. 112). Some SOEs incur losses because the state set prices of their products at below market prices. These include SOEs in such industries as coal, crude oil, electric power, water supply, transportation, and trade. Others are producers of heavy industrial materials and military goods, which now face declining demand for their products. Still others are the numerous

---

[11]About 75 percent of the bad loans of the state banks were loans to SOEs and collective enterprises (Zhao, 2001, p. 7).

[12]Their profits per unit of gross output of industrial SOEs have dropped from 15.5 percent in 1978 to 1.6 percent in 1997. So have profits per unit of capital dropped, from 22.9 to 0.8 percent. Over the same period, the ratio of working capital to gross value of output rose from 32 to 80 percent (SSB, 1985, pp. 125–126; SA 98, p. 112). Likewise, profits per unit of gross output in state-owned construction enterprises dropped from 6.9 to 0.4 percent during 1980–2000 (SSB, 1988, p. 77; SY 01, p. 524). Similar trends are found in railroads and trade.

small factories built by local governments that flood the market with their consumer durables. Most lose money simply because of their poor management, or misuse of funds, e.g., speculating in real estate development and in the stock market. The loss makers often make no effort to repay bank loans, on the grounds that early or late payments should not matter, since both the banks and SOEs are state owned, and therefore these are debts between members of the same family. Some even use irregular means to deliberately evade repayment (*Jingji ribao* [Economic Daily], September 1, 1994, p. 4). The banks, for their part, are reluctant to enforce repayment, partly because bringing the issue into the open would make public the poor quality of their portfolios, partly because the government dis-courages bankrupting the SOEs, and partly because there is yet no effective legal means to recover substantial portions of the loans in bankruptcy proceedings. For all these reasons, bad loans continue to accumulate, even though the loans are being used for wage payments of loss making SOEs or for production of goods that are non-marketable.

Some bad loans result not from policy lending or from the poor performance of SOEs, but from bad management of the banks. The state banks' autonomy in making loans is rather limited. Where they are free to lend, they lack the motivation and the pressure to do so according to commercial principles. Efficiency in the use of funds is unrelated to the interests of the managers or the employees. Like all SOEs, the state banks face soft budget constraints. They are not pe-nalized even when they are overloaded with bad loans. Nor are they forced into bankruptcy when they are insolvent. Thus, they are under no pressure to ensure safe and remunerative use of their funds. If the loans go bad, as many did in financing real estate development in the 1990s, so be it (Zhao, 2001, p. 20).

Another problem is that competition within the banking sector is quite limited. Nonstate banks do exist, including one private bank, branches of foreign banks, and numerous credit cooperatives. But they are relatively small in terms of assets or loans, and their expan-sion has been held back for fear that they might take away too much of the state banks' business. In short, there are no market forces to pressure the state banks to operate more efficiently.

Moreover, long accustomed to policy lending, the state banks have little experience is assessing credit. They are unfamiliar with asset and liquidity management techniques, accounting standards that are needed for performance review and risk assessment, and systems of corporate governance. They are also handicapped by a substandard infrastructure in the banking sector. The quality of the services provided by the banking staff is rather poor because of lack of training (*South China Morning Post*, July 1, 1995, p. B4). The information system is far from adequate for efficient management decisionmaking. The legal framework is so weak that lawlessness both inside and outside the banking sector becomes quite common. As Cheng notes (1999, pp. 15, 20), corruption has been rampant and loan contracts are flouted with impunity. Under all these unfavorable internal and external conditions, commercialization of the state banks is hardly feasible, and bad loans are the inevitable result.

According to a survey by the PBC of the four state banks in 2001, the relative importance of the three main sources of bad loans is as follows: 35 percent originate from policy lending and related causes, 43 percent from poor performance of the SOEs, and 22 percent from mismanagement of the banks (*Xin bao* [Hong Kong Economic Journal], May 17, 2002, p. 11; Zhao, 2001, pp. 19–20). Whether or not these figures accurately reflect the true pattern is really not important to our discussion. What is significant is that reducing and eliminating the three types of bad loans all require formidable reforms. Getting rid of policy loans involves reorienting the functions of the central government away from direct allocation of resources among industries, projects, and firms. It also requires fiscal reforms to remove the local governments' incentive to suboptimize at the regional level, and to relieve the banks of the burden of supporting activities that should be funded through the state budget, e.g., loans to promote "stability and unity." Above all, it calls for strong political will to implement and enforce the many laws and regulations. Furthermore, the debt-ridden SOEs and the state banks themselves badly need enterprise reforms, and perhaps privatization. The point is that these reforms cannot be accomplished overnight. That means the bad loans will be there for some time to come.

If the bad loans are likely to continue to mount, the only alternative for the banks to reduce their fragility is to increase the capital of the banks. Unfortunately, the prospects of improving the state banks' capitalization by their own efforts are rather dim, because they have inadequate loan-loss provisions, because their operating margins and profitability are low, and because their poor credit rating makes it difficult to raise capital in domestic and international financial markets. Prior to 1988, China's banks had no reserves for bad debt. Unrecoverable loans remained on the books as part of bank assets. In 1995, the PBC required all banks to set aside an amount equivalent to 0.8 percent of total loans as provision for bad debt. In 1996, the loan-loss ratio for the five largest banks was only 0.5 percent (*South China Morning Post*, December 21, 1995, p. B5; Cheng, 1999, p. 9). The meager reserves of 0.5 percent of total loans can hardly cover the low official estimate of unrecoverable loans, 2.9 percent (for 1998), not to mention the much higher unofficial estimate of 20 percent (Yuan, 2000, p. 12; Tian and Sun, 1995).

One of the reasons why loss provisions are inadequate is that the state banks' profitability has been declining since the 1980s. The four state banks' returns on assets have dropped markedly from 1.4 percent in 1987 to 0.4 percent in 1996, and further to 0.26 percent in the late 1990s (*The Economist*, May 2, 1998, p. 65; Zhao, 2001, p. 108). The causes of low profitability are many. The policy loans are largely in the nature of grants or subsidies rather than income-generating loans. The banks' poor management is certainly a factor. Another important factor is the government interest rate policy. In China, interest rates on loans and deposits are uniformly set by the PBC. Interest rates on loans have been deliberately kept low, partly to lower the cost of financing SOEs and public projects, and partly to pass the banks' monopoly profits to users of bank credit.[13] Interest rates on deposits cannot be set too low. Otherwise deposits are not forthcoming. The result is a rather narrow spread between the loan and deposit rates.[14]

Just as the rising volume of bad loans and declining profitability continue to deplete the banks' financial resources, structural

---

[13]Some borrowers who have access to bank credit at subsidized rates make money simply by borrowing from the banks and lending to others at high interest rates.

[14]For example, it was only 0.7, 1.1, 2.6 percentage points in 1990, 1995, and 1998, respectively (World Bank, *World Development Report* [WDR], 1994, p. 184; World Bank, 1997g, p. 216; World Bank, *Entering the 21st Century: World Development Report 1999/2000*, Oxford University Press, Oxford, 1999, p. 260).

changes in the financial institutions' assets and liabilities further complicate the banks' liquidity problem. The share of medium- and long-term loans in total bank loans increased sharply, from 2.3 percent in 1980 to 28.1 percent in 2000. Yet, the share of savings deposits in total bank deposits dropped from 62.1 to 49.7 percent over the same period.[15] The use of more and more short-term funds to finance long-term projects increases the risk of a liquidity crunch. This is particularly the case with the state banks, because, to them, deposits represent hard liabilities, whereas their loans to the SOEs are largely soft loans, the repayment of which is rather uncertain.

UNREGULATED FINANCIAL INSTITUTIONS

One distinct feature of China's rapid economic growth since the early 1980s is that it was led by the rise of the nonstate enterprises. Toward the end of the 1990s, these enterprises were facing increasing difficulties in getting adequate funds from the banking system, mainly because of the government's strong bias against them in allocating credit. They therefore have to seek financing outside the banking sector, from such sources as capital markets, investment trusts, inter-enterprise lending, and the informal financial sector.

Throughout the 1990s, capital markets remained underdeveloped and poorly regulated. They served mainly as channels for the government to finance public projects or investment of the SOEs. Nonstate enterprises have only limited access.[16] In any case, total funds raised in the stock and bond markets have been relatively small.[17] This is mainly because the government keeps a tight rein over the listing of stocks on the main boards or the floating of bonds, ostensibly to protect the investors, but apparently also to regulate the scale of nonbank borrowing and to ensure consistency of the flow of financial resources with government industrial policies (Ma, 1993, p. 2).

---

[15]SSB, 1999, pp. 64, 66; SY 01, pp. 304, 637–638.

[16]Thus, only a handful of the 1,000-odd companies listed in China's two stock exchanges are privately controlled (*The Economist*, June 30, 2002, p. 72).

[17]In 2000, they amounted to only 14 percent of the total funds provided by financial institutions and capital markets in China (SA 01, pp. 78, 82).

Notwithstanding stringent government control, irregular borrowing in pseudo-capital markets has been rampant. Many enterprises issued shares for sale to their own employees and the public. Others sold securities with fixed returns under various names, but not as bonds, so as to bypass the procedure of having the securities assessed and approved by the authorities (*Ming pao*, September 12, 1985, p. 8; *Liaowang* [Outlook], No. 16, April 19, 1993, p. 3; *Jingji ribao* [Economic Daily], September 4, 1994, p. 5). The practice was not limited to borrowing by enterprises. Many government organizations and public institutions, like hospitals and schools, also actively raised funds from their employees, sometimes on a compulsory basis (*China Daily*, April 24, 1993, p. 4).

In both the formal and pseudo-formal capital markets, the regulatory framework is rather weak. The Shanghai and the Shenzhen exchanges are plagued by price manipulation and poor oversight (WSJ, February 24, 2000, p. A14). Insiders' trading of issues on the main boards is not uncommon. Many enterprises have to pay interest rates as high as 20–30 percent per annum, several times the bank rate for savings deposits (*Liaowang*, No. 18, May 3, 1993, p. 17). Few companies can guarantee to make that much profits year after year. Defaults on the loans often result.

Another source of finance outside the banking sector is the investment and trust companies (ITCs), which were developed to raise funds from foreign and domestic creditors. Since the 1980s, ITCs have proliferated, as local governments, particularly those in the coastal provinces, strived hard to attract foreign investments. Just as in the case of other financial institutions, strict regulations governing the operations of the ITCs exist but are only loosely enforced. A survey of hundreds of ITCs in 1985 revealed that more than one-third did not have sufficient capital, did not maintain adequate minimum reserves, and violated lending and interest rate regulations (Holz, 1992, pp. 116–117). Many invested in ill-advised projects and became debt ridden.[18] Subsequently, the government decided to restructure

---

[18]By 2000, it was estimated that the trust firms had bad debts totaling US$ 25 billion, while less than half of their assets, US$ 50 billion, were recoverable (WSJ, February 16, 2000, p. A23). In 1998, Guangdong International Trust and Investment Corporation failed. It had only US$ 785 million in assets, against US$ 4,700 million in liabilities (WSJ, September 2, 1999, p. A18).

and shut down more than 150 of the 240 debt-ridden ITCs through mergers and closures. Once again, China's experience with the ITCs points to a critical problem in the financial system. Like the banks, ITCs apparently have little difficulty in raising funds, but they lack the expertise and prudence in managing the funds.

A third type of nonbank financial institution includes those in the informal sector, such as private lending among individuals and enterprises, money shops and loan brokers, traditional credit unions, farmers' cooperative funds, pawn shops, and unlicensed private banks (Deng and Xu, 1994, pp. 110–117; *China Daily*, November 7, 1992, p. 1). Some of these institutions operate primarily for profit (e.g., loan brokers), while others provide financial help to the needy (e.g., mutual aid funds). Some are legal (e.g., the farmers' cooperative funds), while others are not (e.g., money shops and unlicensed private banks). By some guesses, the informal sector provided half the credit in the economy in the early 1990s (*The Economist*, July 3, 1993, p. 30). Thus, informal financial institutions thrive in the coastal provinces such as Guangdong, Zhejiang, and Fujian where nonstate enterprises flourish. Some local governments at the village and county level overspend and have to borrow from the informal sector (Yang, 1997, pp. 146–149). Then there are people who borrow to finance conspicuous consumption (*Wen hui pao*, August 7, 1990, p. 10).

The major suppliers of funds are the individuals with savings who seek better returns in curb markets where interest rates are much higher than bank deposit rates.[19] To some degree, the supply of funds in these markets relieved the acute shortage of capital for the nonstate enterprises. In that sense, it helps to sustain economic growth. But it also creates some problems. Because the informal sector is little regulated and supervised, it has become a hot bed for financial disputes. If and when these projects fail, the lenders cannot always recoup funds, because some loans are illegal, and, even if they are legal, the underdeveloped legal system provides no protection. Sometimes, the lenders resort to force to collect their debts, creating problems of law and order. If and when the local governments can-

---

[19]For example, the curb market rate in 1993 was 40 percent per annum, compared to the bank fixed deposit rate of 11 percent (one year period) (*The Economist*, March 18, 1995, p. S16; SY 98, p. 671).

not pay their debts, they often shift the burden to the peasants by increasing arbitrary levies, creating strong resentments among the public (Yang, 1997, pp. 148–149).

ADVERSE SCENARIOS: FINANCIAL CRISES AND SLACK ECONOMIC GROWTH

With an ineffectual central bank, a highly fragile banking system, and nonbank institutions lacking an effective regulatory framework, the stage is set for potential financial crises. A number of abrupt changes in the economic and social environment could trigger a financial crisis. Earlier, we noted that the insolvent state banks have been keeping the insolvent SOEs afloat with unrecoverable loans. Thus far, the perverse one-way drain of the banks' resources has not brought on a financial crisis, because the supply of bank funds from its two main sources has been readily forthcoming: growth of deposits and central bank lending. Nonetheless, that the system has not collapsed does not signify the absence of a crisis risk. The State Council controls central bank lending, and it is unlikely to turn off the tap unless absolutely necessary. Deposits are a different matter. In the past two decades, bank deposits have been growing rapidly through good and bad times. This is because the depositors believe that the government would always stand behind the state banks. However, policies can change under pressure, and so can people's perceptions.

One such possibility is a crisis originating in the informal sector. Because the curb lending rates are high—some 20–30 percent per annum—borrowing occurs to finance projects with relatively high expected returns, which often have high risks, such as speculations in real estate and stock markets. The weak regulatory framework could not stop a financial bubble from growing, and if a large number of these projects fail, the lenders would be in trouble, because the state would probably not come to their rescue. A crisis in the informal sector could spread to the formal sector through the contagion of fear and a rush for liquidity by the bank depositors.

Another potential trigger of financial crises is a loss of confidence of the domestic savers in the government's guarantee of the value of their bank deposits. This could occur when the real interest rate drops sharply because of high inflation. To protect the real value of their savings, people might withdraw their deposits and shift into real assets. A bank run would then ensue (Lardy, 1998, pp. 201–202). This actually happened in 1988. The incident was brief and did not develop into a full-scale crisis because the government quickly introduced index-based deposits to keep the real interest rate from falling, while taking other measures to curb inflation. As will be pointed out presently, the risk of recurring inflation is there, and we cannot preclude the possibility of people running away from financial assets to avoid the inflation tax.

Similarly, a run from the domestic currency could occur, as a result of political and social turmoil, military conflicts, or competitive devaluation among China's trading partners and rivals. China has been able to avert serious consequences of the Asian financial crisis of 1997–1998. But this does not mean that the financial system is immune to external shocks, especially now that China has joined the World Trade Organization and the economy will become increasingly integrated with the outside world.

Even if no financial crisis occurs, the basic weaknesses of the financial system could stifle economic growth through their negative effects on inflation, savings, and efficiency in the use of financial resources. Our discussions of the nature and causes of China's financial problems indicate that many of China's financial difficulties are, in effect, the price that government elected to pay for postponing fiscal and enterprise reforms. China faces persistent budget deficits, mainly because the tax system fails to increase revenues fast enough to cover the mounting expenditures on defense, subsidies, debt service, environmental protection, and institutional building. Increasingly, the government relies on the state banks to finance public investments, welfare expenditures, and subsidies to loss-making SOEs. By shouldering these fiscal burdens, the banks help to reduce the risks of state budget crunch, wholesale SOE bankruptcies, and massive open unemployment. The cost is that the PBC loses control of money supply, because these noneconomic demands for bank credit are inflexible and constantly expanding. The loans to the ailing SOEs are often used to pay wages or to produce unmarketable goods. The result is an increase in aggregate demand without a corresponding increase in aggregate supply. In addition, the priority goal of the central and local governments is economic growth, and the banks are under great pressure to support government development policies. Under the circumstances, high inflation could recur as it did in the 1980s and 1990s.

An empirical study of inflation and economic growth based on data for 122 countries has shown that the effect of inflation on growth is significantly negative (Barro, 1998, pp. 89–118). Such adverse effects could happen in China. For example, inflation could deter investment because it increases risks of investment decisions. A high rate of inflation suggests that the government has lost macroeconomic control. There would be uncertainties regarding the political will of the leaders to control inflation, the measures they might take, and the effectiveness of these measures. In times of inflation, volatile relative prices do not convey signals of changing supply and demand by producers and consumers. More often than not, enterprise managers are more interested in rent-seeking through short-term speculation than in making profits through long-term investments.

Moreover, inflation has important distributional effects. Real income is shifted from those with fixed incomes, such as workers and employees, to those whose incomes vary with inflation, such as entrepreneurs and holders of physical or foreign assets. In China, the former group is fairly large. In 2000, 53 percent of the total urban workforce were workers and employees (SA 01, pp. 41–42). To the extent that income changes affect work incentives, inflation could reduce the effective labor input from the large number of workers and employees. Worse still, discontent among workers and employees could degenerate into social upheavals.

Apart from the negative effects of inflation, the financial system's weaknesses could slow economic growth through their adverse effects on the supply of savings and on the efficiency of resource allocation. In the past two decades, domestic savings have played a major role in the rapid economic growth. However, since 1993, the investment rate has continually declined, from 43.5 percent in 1993 to 36.9 percent in 2000 (SA 01, p. 28). The domestic savings rate must have declined even more sharply, because net foreign lending and direct foreign investment have been rising during the period (SA 01, p. 156). The rising volume of the state banks' bad loans might well have contributed to the decline. As a source of total bank funds, household savings deposits have become increasingly important, rising from 8.2 percent of total assets in 1978 to 43.4 percent in 2000

(SSB, 1999, p. 64; Almanac, 2001, p. 360). Meanwhile, the SOEs absorbed 82.8 percent of state bank lending in 1998 (Holz and Zhu, 2000, p. 76). A considerable proportion of these loans is unrecoverable. In short, large sums of household savings have been channeled to the insolvent SOEs through the state banks. The process could escalate to a crisis if, for some reason, households should decide to save less or to shift their savings elsewhere. Even if no crisis occurs, the process could drain the banks' loanable resources, because lending to the SOEs is a one-way flow of funds into a bottomless pit. The banks' capacity to support healthy projects could thus be greatly reduced, restricting the growth of investment. Among those that suffer the most from such constraints would be the nonstate enterprises. These enterprises happen to be the more productive units in the economy. The credit squeeze on a more efficient sector represents a misallocation of financial resources that lowers the growth of total factor productivity.

The shortcomings of the financial system could also impede economic growth through the system's effects on the structure of investment. We note earlier that inflation could recur because of the ineffectual central bank. With nominal interest rates set by the government at low levels, inflation could depress the real interest rate to near or subzero levels, as it did in 1988–1989 and 1993–1995. Negative interest rates could make capital-intensive investments appear more attractive. Large investments based on illusions of low capital costs could have dire consequences. They could worsen the problem of existing massive unemployment, because the number of jobs created per unit of investment would be lower than in the case of labor-intensive investments. If these capital-intensive industries should face strong competition in domestic or world markets from enterprises with more truly favorable comparative advantages, they could go under and tie up scarce resources indefinitely, just as the "third-line" industries did in the past.[20]

As in the case of massive unemployment, we roughly quantify the effects of a deteriorating financial system, first, by using the World Bank's model of sustained growth as a benchmark, and then by al-

---

[20]Third-line industries are those built in the mountainous areas in the interior of China during the 1960s and 1970s in preparation for war.

lowing for changes in the parameters due to the worsening of the financial problems. In the World Bank model, the projected GDP growth rate of 6.6 percent is decomposed into three contributing factors: a 35 percent investment rate that contributes 4.6 percentage points to GDP growth, labor inputs growing at 0.8 percent per year that generate 0.5 percentage points to GDP growth, and total factor productivity growing at 1.5 percent per year.[21]

In the two adverse scenarios, we postulate a discernible drop in the investment rate from 35 to 33 and 30 percent, mainly as a result of a slowdown in the growth of the banks' resources that are available for investment, as the banks' subsidies to the ailing SOEs continue to expand, and as depositors and investors become increasingly concerned over the financial health of the economic system. We also assume a decline in the growth of employment from 0.8 to 0.7 and 0.6 percent, to provide a range of possible changes. Total factor productivity also falls from 1.5 to 1.3 and 1.2 percent, mainly as a consequence of the government's diverting the bulk of financial resources to the less productive state sector, thus constraining the growth of the more dynamic nonstate sector. Given these assumptions, the projected GDP growth drops to 6.1 and 5.6 percent. In short, the deteriorating financial system could set back economic growth by 0.5 to 1.0 percentage points.

---

[21]For sources of data, see Chapter Two.

Chapter Eight

POSSIBLE SHRINKAGE OF FOREIGN CAPITAL INFLOWS

INTRODUCTION: SOME RELEVANT BACKGROUND

China is currently the world's second largest recipient of foreign direct investment (FDI); the largest is the United States. Private capital flows into China currently represent about 40 percent of all foreign capital flows in emerging market economies.

From 1985 to 2000, FDI in China increased from an annual rate of $2 billion in the mid-1980s to over $40 billion in 2001. Three observations should be added:

1. The increase in FDI from 1986 to 1997 was monotonic, although the rate of increase declined in the latter part of that period.

2. Since 1998, FDI in China has slightly declined in real terms.

3. For the period from 1985 through 2000, the annual compound rate of growth in real FDI was 18.5 percent.

Table 8.1 shows China's GDP and the volume of *disbursed* FDI in China from 1985 to 2001 in then-year dollars and in constant 1995 dollars.[1]

---

[1]The figures in Table 8.1 represent disbursed FDI as contrasted with "contracted" FDI: The latter is typically higher than the former because contracted amounts sometimes do not fully materialize in the specified year nor, for that matter, even in subsequent

Table 8.1

Gross Domestic Product and Foreign Direct Investment in China, 1985–2001
(billions of current and constant 1995 dollars)

Year	GDP Current Prices (billions of RMB)	GDP Constant Prices (billions of 1995 RMB)	GDP Constant Dollar Prices (billions of 1995 US$)	FDI (billions of US$)	FDI (billions of constant 1995 US$)
1984	716	1956	236		
1985	879	2273	274		
1986	1013	2475	298	2.2	2.9
1987	1178	2761	333	2.3	2.9
1988	1470	3072	370	3.2	3.9
1989	1647	3197	385	3.4	4.0
1990	1832	3320	400	3.5	4.0
1991	2128	3625	437	4.4	4.8
1992	2586	4141	499	11.0	11.7
1993	3450	4700	566	27.5	28.6
1994	4669	5295	638	33.8	34.5
1995	5851	5851	705	37.5	37.5
1996	6833	6412	773	41.7	40.9
1997	7490	6977	841	45.3	43.6
1998	7985	7521	906	45.5	43.3
1999	8205	8056	971	40.3	37.7
2000	8940	8700	1048	40.7	37.3
2001				21.6[a]	

SOURCES: International Monetary Fund, *International Financial Statistics*, Washington, D.C., September 2001; SSB, 2001.

[a]This figure is for the first six months of 2001.

Among China specialists as well as many business and financial observers, the consensus is that (1) FDI is important for China's continued economic growth (not necessarily *more* important than several other influences, but nevertheless highly important), and (2) the amount of FDI is sensitive to domestic and international circumstances.[2] In this chapter, we address both aspects of this consensus:

---

years. Dollar figures have been converted to 1995 constant dollars using the U.S. GDP deflator.

[2]See Wendy Dobson and Gary C. Hufbauer, *World Capital Markets*, Institute for International Economics, Washington, D.C., 2001; Hu Angang, "The Chinese Economy in Prospect," in Shuxun Chen and Charles Wolf, Jr., eds., *China, The United States, and the Global Economy*, RAND, Santa Monica, Calif., MR-1300-RC, 2001, Chapter Six, pp.

In the next section, the focus is on the second point: namely, those influences that might cause FDI to rise or to shrink appreciably. Later we focus on the first point: the effects of a possible shrinkage in FDI on China's future economic growth.

WHAT WILL AFFECT FDI IN CHINA IN THE 2002–2010 PERIOD?

The circumstances that would tend to boost FDI in China are the same factors whose absence or deterioration would shrink it, although the magnitudes of the upward and downward effects may not be symmetric. For example, the deleterious effect of conflict in the Taiwan Strait would greatly exceed the buoyant effect of peaceful relations between the mainland and Taiwan.

A survey conducted by the authors in February 2002 among several dozen putative China experts with self-declared general familiarity with the subject yielded the following results: (1) 88 percent of those responding conjectured that the average annual rate of FDI in China would rise over the period from 2002 to 2010, while 12 percent conjectured that it would fall. (2) Of those opining that FDI would rise, 38 percent thought the increases would be "small" (i.e., less than $3 billion[3] annually), an equal proportion thought the increase would be "moderate" (greater than $3 billion but less than $8 billion), and 12 percent thought the increase would be "large" (greater than $8 billion); the respondents who conjectured that FDI would fall, opined that the fall would be "small."

The magnitude of FDI in China will be influenced by both *internal* and *external* circumstances.

The Internal Political and Economic Environment

Just as a smooth *leadership succession*, in which Hu Jintao and associates harmoniously replace Jiang Zemin as China's president along with Jiang's associates, would reassure and encourage foreign in-

---

99–146; and Angus Maddison, *Chinese Economic Performance in the Long-Run*, OECD, Paris, 1998.

[3]All dollar amounts are in U.S. dollars.

vestment, so too would an uneven, dissonant, and frictional succession discourage it. The precise tonality of the succession process may not be evident during the initial transitional period in which apparent tranquillity might conceal subsurface frictions, or at least ripples. Such an uncertain transition, let alone a manifestly unstable one, would enhance uncertainty and discourage direct investment.

Intensified *political and social unrest*—reflected perhaps in large-scale public demonstrations, vandalism, or violence—might ensue in China either in relation to a conflicted leadership transition or, indeed, independent of it. For example, unrest might be a widespread reaction to the imposition of fees or other arbitrary exactions imposed by cadres and local officials, or as a result of seriously rising unemployment especially in urban areas, or as a consequence of public revulsion against corrupt practices among political elites.[4] Whatever its source, such unrest would make the environment for foreign investment less hospitable, resulting in a big increase in the risk premium for FDI, and a shrinkage in its volume.

Another source of potential impedance of foreign investment is a possible further deterioration in China's *internal financial system*. China's largest financial institutions are the Bank of China and the three other state-owned banks for industry, construction, and agriculture. The balance sheets of these institutions are riddled with nonperforming loans that have accumulated in large volume through years of "policy lending" to perennially loss-incurring SOEs.[5] As a result, the solvency of these institutions is precarious, as it has been for some time. While China's huge annual savings (over 35 percent of GDP) provide an ample flow of deposits, it is by no means implausible that a run on these banks might ensue, creating a financial panic throughout the economy. The resulting adverse effect on foreign investment could be both large and persistent, even if the initial period of panic were limited in duration.

Separate from, although not entirely unrelated to, the precarious balance sheets of the state-owned banks is the recurrence of *financial scandals*, such as that associated with the Bank of China, which

---

[4]See Chapter Two, above.

[5]See Chapter Seven, above.

is the most internationally oriented of China's large banks. This scandal and others that may be in the pipeline would have a further depressing effect on foreign direct investment.

In the Bank of China case, a two-year investigation by the U.S. Treasury's Controller of the Currency, with the cooperation of Chinese regulators, exposed a record of fraudulent loans, preferential lending terms extended to favored borrowers, and other corrupt practices.[6] The subsequent removal of the BOC president from his position, and the evident cooperation provided by Chinese regulators in the investigation and in the levying of the $20 million penalty on the BOC, may have a partially redemptive effect on the environment for future investment. Such a damage-limiting effect will depend, of course, on whether these developments signal that more rigorous oversight and preventive measures will be applied in the future. However, this mitigating effect may not be sufficient to allay the fears of potential foreign investors lest they become squeezed by corrupt practices if and when they acquire illiquid assets in China, resulting in a serious deterrent to future foreign investments.

The recent BOC scandal is one example among many of the limited reach of the rule of the law whose effect is to render the economic environment less predictable, less appealing, and more risky to foreign investors.

One experienced observer has referred to the congeries of institutions that contribute to effective markets and facilitate economic transactions as a "nation's economic infrastructure . . . [which] is no less important than the system of highways, railways, etc. which make up the transportation infrastructure."[7] China's shortcomings in this domain are a major impediment to foreign investment, which may in the future cause it to shrink.

A country's *economic infrastructure* includes enforcement of contracts and other aspects of property rights; probity and predictability

---

[6]See Matt Pottinger, "Bank of China Reaches Deal with the U.S.," WSJ, January 18, 2002; and Matt Pottinger, "Banker's Fall Symbolizes China's Flaws," WSJ, January 21, 2002.

[7]Jerry L. Jordan, *The U.S. Economy, Monetary Policy, and Essentials for Prosperity,* paper delivered at the Fourth Annual RAND–China Reform Forum Conference, Santa Monica, Calif., November 29–30, 2001.

of the judicial system in resolving disputes; and competence and objectivity of internal and, especially, external auditing in conformity with rigorous, explicit, and transparent accounting standards. Similarly, the quality and competence of monetary and fiscal policies and institutions, and of the central banking system, are other key aspects of the economic infrastructure to which foreign investors are sensitive.

As the recent abysmal failure of Enron in the United States demonstrates, the economic infrastructures of developed countries also sometimes fall far below the standards to which they aspire. China's infrastructural deficiencies present formidable obstacles to creating and sustaining an economic environment that is congenial to foreign investment.

The president of the Federal Reserve Bank of Cleveland, Dr. Jerry Jordan, concludes his discourse on economic infrastructure, with the following admonition:

> When the institutional arrangements of a country [i.e., its economic infrastructure] are not stable and predictable, economic performance suffers as much as or more than when policies are erratic and unpredictable.[8]

To be sure, all of these ingredients are acknowledged by China's top leadership to be important elements in China's economic reform.[9] Another important element is the modernization, regulation, and enhancement of China's hitherto dysfunctional securities markets, and the only modestly successful efforts of China's Securities and Regulatory Commission to instill improvements in corporate governance of companies listed on these markets.[10] If and as these institutional reforms progress, the environment for FDI in China would become increasingly congenial. By the same token, if these efforts falter, stagnate, or are reversed—scenarios that are not entirely

---

[8]Ibid., p. 6.

[9]See statement by Premier Zhu Rongji, *Report on the Work of the Government*, at the opening of the Fifth Session of the Ninth National People's Congress, Beijing, March 5, 2002.

[10]See Charles Wolf, Jr., "Capitalism, Chinese Style," *International Economy*, Washington, D.C., Winter 2002.

implausible—the internal environment will be viewed by foreign investors as unfavorable, and perhaps hostile, to foreign investment.[11]

If such adverse developments ensue, two consequences would follow: First, FDI would shrink perhaps precipitously; and second, such FDI as occurs would require a substantial premium in expected yields to compensate for the added risk associated with the adversities engendered by China's economic infrastructure. Further down the road, harvesting of these yields by foreign investors could generate hostile political reactions from Chinese nationalists, which, in turn, would have negative repercussions for further foreign investment.

China's *membership in the World Trade Organization* (WTO) should encourage foreign investors—especially if and when the WTO and its members embrace a planned Multilateral Agreement on Investment code to which all members subscribe. Whether and when this will actually occur is uncertain.

In completing its five-year process of qualifying for WTO membership, China concluded some 900 pages of bilateral agreements with other WTO members (among the most voluminous agreements were those with the European Union and the United States). These agreements involve pledges to lower tariffs by specified rates, as well as to provide greater access by foreign investors in financial services, insurance, legal services, and telecommunications. If these pledges are fully complied with, the effect on FDI would surely be positive. But if, as is not unlikely, *China's compliance lags* significantly—a pattern that other WTO members have demonstrated in the past—a severe shrinkage of FDI could occur.

To be sure, a slow pace of lowering tariffs and liberalizing nontariff barriers might provide a positive incentive for FDI to get inside protectionist barriers. On the other hand, if administrative restrictions confronting foreign investors—as distinct from explicit and visible tariff reductions—were to increase, the result may be to circumscribe

---

[11]For a view that accords high probability, rather than just "plausibility" to such adverse developments, see Gordon Chang, *The Coming Collapse of China*, Random House, New York, 2001.

opportunities accessible to foreign investors in the services fields mentioned above, with a corresponding dampening effect on FDI.[12]

A final and major influence on foreign investment is the *convertibility and stability of China's currency.* To some extent these two attributes are in conflict with one another. China's yuan has, indeed, been the most stable of Asia's currencies in the past half-dozen years, maintaining a value of between 8.2 and 8.28 renminbi (RMB) per U.S. dollar throughout the period.

However, while the RMB is convertible at this rate on current account, it is nonconvertible on capital account. This is plainly a disincentive for particular types of foreign investment: namely, those targeted on production and sales for China's potentially huge domestic market. Such investments aim at net revenues over costs in RMB. Hence, uncertainty as to whether and on what terms RMB profits will be convertible into dollars or other foreign currencies can be a significant impediment to investment in sectors and industries focused on domestic sales within China.

In sum, a wide range of plausible internal developments in China could seriously vitiate the environment for foreign investment: friction in the transition from China's old to its new leadership, civil unrest perhaps triggered by increased unemployment, financial crisis resulting from the large and growing volume of nonperforming loans on the balance sheets of China's main banks, financial and other scandals in the Chinese business and financial environment, failure to develop the legal and financial infrastructure on which foreign investment especially depends, noncompliance with WTO commitments, and inconvertibility of RMB earnings. While any of these developments would influence the risk premium associated with FDI and, hence, would affect its volume, a clustering of several of them could plausibly lead to a major shrinkage of FDI, perhaps by as much as one-half or two-thirds of the recent flow, e.g., over $42 billion in 2001. In light of the legacy of Asia's financial crisis of 1997–1998, this

---

[12]There have been some indications that China may be embarking on such restrictive regulations. For example, foreign financial institutions in China are required to maintain 60 percent of their registered capital in local currency at local branches, thereby disbursing capital and probably boosting operating costs. Law firms will also be required to wait a year before they can demonstrate a "need for establishing" a physical office presence in China. See WSJ, February 5, 2002.

conjecture about the elasticity of FDI with respect to these clustered changes is as likely to be too low as too high.

External Influences on FDI in China

International capital markets have been important, as well as highly volatile, elements in the global economy in the past five centuries, since the Portuguese, Dutch, British, French, and Spanish colonial ventures in Asia, the Middle East, and the Americas.[13] The markets have in recent decades become increasingly integrated, open, and competitive, except for occasional interruptions by periodic financial crises, such as those occurring in Asia in 1997–1998, Russia in 1999, and Brazil in 2000. Nevertheless, according to some metrics, the degree of integration in global capital markets was actually *greater* at the end of the 19th century and prior to World War I than in recent years.[14]

Because of the increased integration of global capital markets, FDI in China will be determined by the risk-adjusted, after-tax rate of return on assets accessible to acquisition by foreign investors in China, compared with similar rates of return on assets in the rest of the world—notably, in emerging markets in East Asia, India, Southwest Asia, the Middle East, Russia, Eastern Europe, and Latin America, as well as in Western Europe and the United States. Notwithstanding the storied lure of China's potentially enormous market (note that India's is potentially of near equal size), FDI in China will rise if and as the risks of investment fall and rates of return rise in China relative to those elsewhere, including the competitive risk-adjusted rates of return *within* the capital exporting countries themselves.

Equivalently, FDI in China would fall—perhaps deeply and perhaps abruptly—if and as the risk-adjusted rates of return on assets accessible to foreign investors in China fall relative to the opportunities available, or in the process of becoming available, elsewhere.

---

[13]See Wendy Dobson and Gary C. Hufbauer, *World Capital Markets*, Institute for International Economics, Washington, D.C., 2001; and Kevin O'Rourke and Jeffrey Williamson, *Globalization and History*, MIT Press, Cambridge, Mass., 1999.

[14]See Charles Wolf, Jr., "Globalization: Meaning and Measurement," *Critical Review*, April 2001.

The factors within China that could drive a relative decline of FDI were summarized in the preceding section. In the *rest of the world*, especially in other emerging markets, factors similar to those cited in the previous section could enhance confidence in and returns from FDI in these other areas. *Competitive efforts in other developing countries* to create and/or strengthen their legal or financial infrastructure, their practices of corporate governance, and their political and social stability and predictability could enhance their drawing power for foreign investment compared to that of China. *New resource discoveries* in other areas—such as may impend in the central Asian republics—are another wild card in the competitive game for mobile and global capital.

Finally, adverse changes in *China's relations with its neighbors* (including Taiwan, and with ethnic Chinese in Southeast Asia), as well as with the United States, Japan, the European Union, and India, would also shrink FDI in China over the 2002–2010 period. At the upper end of this spectrum of possible adversities, and also at the intersection of external and internal drivers of FDI in China, would be a serious confrontation in the Taiwan Strait. If the Taiwan situation were to escalate from the present relatively quiescent position to hostile rhetoric, to serious tension, to embargoes in the strait, and to direct military confrontation, FDI could be expected to decline along with, but probably more abruptly than, movement to each successive rung in this escalation ladder.

For example, the effects of a missile-imposed embargo on trade in the strait would so sharply boost insurance premiums for cargo shipping that incentives for foreign investment in China would sharply decline, as would the volume of trade transactions with China. The resulting chill this would impart to foreign investors could be short- or long-lived, more probably the latter. Even if the near-term effect were intended to be once and for all, it is extremely doubtful this intention would encourage some investors more than it would discourage others.

Just as *conflict in the Taiwan Strait* would have a seriously depressant effect on FDI in China, so would *conflicts elsewhere in Asia*—for example, on the Korean peninsula—tend to discourage foreign investment in China, although the repercussions would be less severe than those resulting from contingencies arising in and over the Taiwan Strait.

EFFECTS OF FDI ON CHINA'S ECONOMIC GROWTH

Two Mechanisms

While economists within and outside China generally agree that FDI is important for China's economic growth,[15] there are two different views of the mechanisms that drive FDI's contribution to growth.

The more widely prevalent view is that FDI's special role derives from its unique combination of capital together with technology, management, and marketing skills and linkages—in the latter case relating especially to the promotion of exports to the countries from which foreign investment originates.[16]

A minority view, but one increasingly supported by evidence presented by Professor Yasheng Huang, is that the special importance of FDI derives from quite different sources: namely, imperfect capital mobility within China, resulting from internal barriers to the flow of savings and capital across province lines, as well as tax advantages provided to foreign investors.[17] For example, in the special economic zones on China's east coast, applicable tax rates are less for foreign investors than for domestic investors, although this advantage may be ending as a consequence of China's admission to the WTO and the implicit obligation to apply national treatment to all investors, domestic as well as foreign. This unusual effect might result because application of the national-treatment rule—assuming this applies no

---

[15]See section above, Introduction: Some Relevant Background.

[16]See Dobson and Hufbauer, 2001, op. cit. A recent study of five East Asian countries (Indonesia, Korea, Malaysia, the Philippines, and Thailand) found that companies with a "substantial foreign ownership share have markedly higher productivity than those that are domestically owned," Mary Hallward-Driemeier, Guiseppe Iarossi, and Kenneth Sôkoloff, *Exports and Manufacturing Productivity in East Asia: A Comparative Analysis of Firm-Level Data,* National Bureau of Economic Research Working Paper, No. 8894, Cambridge, Mass., 2002.

[17]See Yasheng Huang, "The Role of Foreign-Invested Enterprises in the Chinese Economy: An Institutional Approach," in Shuxun Chen and Charles Wolf, Jr., eds., *China, The United States, and the Global Economy*, RAND, Santa Monica, Calif., MR-1300-RC, 2001, pp. 147–191.

less to the Multilateral Agreement on Investment that WTO is formulating than it does to trade transactions—will help encourage domestic investment, which has been disfavored, rather than foreign investment, which has been favored in the past.

One effect of the favorable treatment accorded to foreign investment has been the phenomenon of "round tripping," in which domestic Chinese capital has temporarily migrated abroad in order to acquire the special benefits conferred on "foreign" investors when capital is repatriated.

Although the two views are different, and have different implications, both may be valid. However, the effects of a curtailment of FDI on China's economic growth would differ depending on which of the views one adopts or emphasizes. Suppose one adopts the first view about the link between FDI, technology, management, and marketing. In this case, shrinkage of FDI—whether for exogenous reasons, such as the emergence of more attractive investment opportunities elsewhere in the world economy, or for endogenous reasons, such as increasing corruption in China or further deterioration in the rule of law—would mean that China not only would lose the benefit of the reduced foreign capital itself, but would be deprived of the associated benefits of technology, management, and marketing, as well.

If, on the other hand, one adopts the second view—and if in the course of China's further economic reform, internal barriers to capital flows are reduced or eliminated and preferential treatment of foreign investors is removed—then the effect on China's economic growth of diminished FDI might be offset in whole or in part by an increase in the quantity or productivity of domestic investment.

Effects on Growth

In the informal survey of several knowledgeable China experts referred to earlier,[18] opinions were solicited on a multiple-choice basis concerning the conjectured effects of possible changes in FDI on China's economic growth in the 2002–2010 period. Sixty-two percent of the respondents thought that the effects would be "small" (less

---

[18]See above section, What Will Affect FDI in China in the 2002–2010 Period?

than 0.5 percent per year), and 38 percent thought the effects would be "moderate" (between 0.5 and 1 percent per year); none thought the effects would be large (greater than 0.5 percent annually).

Attempting to quantify the effects of changes in foreign direct investment in China on subsequent economic growth is difficult. One difficulty is that, theoretically, the FDI variable we should be looking at is the *stock* of FDI, rather than its annual flow. Information on the accumulated FDI stock is unreliable, for many reasons, including because data are not available on the appropriate depreciation rate to apply to the original FDI, and because it is unknown how to attribute the net FDI stock to its true market value. Estimating these parameters would be arbitrary. Moreover, the extent to which some parts of the accumulated stock of FDI may have been liquidated—for example, by overvaluation of imports, or undervaluation of exports—would be particularly elusive.

Furthermore, numerous other covariates, occurring contemporaneously with FDI, also affect economic performance, thereby confounding the effects that might be attributable to FDI in influencing China's economic growth. Among these covariates are domestic private and public investment; government fiscal, monetary, and regulatory policies; exports and imports; changes in visible or administrative barriers to capital mobility within China; and so on. While some of these confounding variables might be allowed by using suitable dummy variables, or in some cases (i.e., for domestic investment, exports, and imports) by using available data, limitations of both time and budget have precluded our undertaking the more comprehensive model-building that this would require. In any event, the results from doing this would probably still be mired in uncertainty, because of the data problems previously mentioned.

Recognizing these problems, we base our calculations on linear regressions of GDP growth on annual flows of FDI for the period from 1986 through 2001, and, alternatively, on FDI as a fraction of GDP, in both cases with a time variable to allow separately for time trends:[19]

---

[19]Both specifications have been used in other work that explores the relation between FDI and economic growth in developing countries. For example, see Dobson and Hufbauer (2001, op. cit.) and E. Borensztein, J. DeGregorio, and J.-W. Lee, "How Does

$$\text{GDP growth rate} = a_1 (FDI_t) + a_2 T + \text{constant} \qquad (1)$$

$$\text{GDP growth rate} = b_1 (FDI_t/GDP_t) + b_2 T + \text{constant} \qquad (2)$$

where t refers to annual values for GDP and FDI from 1985 through 2001, and T refers to the individual years.

The regression coefficients in Equation 1 for a_1 are 0.0016 (SE = 0.0011), and for a_2, –0.006 (SE = 0.0045), R^2 = 0.13. The coefficients in Equation 2 for b_1 are 1.0046 (SE = 0.7670), and for b_2, –0.0039 (SE = 0.0032), R^2 = 0.15.

It is worth noting that several of the possibly "confounding" variables mentioned above that might be expected to affect GDP growth but have been omitted from these equations—for example, exports, regulatory policies, and protection of property rights—may have evolved steadily over time; consequently, they may be plausibly proxied by the time variable, T, in these equations.

These estimates must be treated with caution because of the uncertainties they entail, as indicated by the high standard errors and the relatively small proportion (13–15 percent) of the variance in GDP growth that they explain. Nevertheless, the results are suggestive and are roughly consistent with other attempts using similarly simple models to make quantitative estimates of the effects of foreign direct investments on economic performance in other developing countries.[20]

While recognizing the uncertainties of the coefficients, it can be conjectured from Equation 1 that a reduction of $1 billion in FDI inflow would reduce annual GDP growth by 0.16 percent, and a reduction of FDI by $10 billion would lower the annual GDP growth rate by 1.6 percent. Correspondingly, a reduction of the FDI/GDP ratio by 1 percent according to Equation 2 would lower the GDP growth rate by 1.0046 percent. This result is generally consistent with

---

Foreign Direct Investment Affect Economic Growth?" *Journal of International Economics*, Vol. 45, 1998.

[20]Borensztein, DeGregorio, and Lee, 1998, found that for 69 developing countries during the period from 1970 to 1989, regressions with similar specifications to those used above resulted in a coefficient for the FDI inflow ratio to GDP of 0.0066, with a standard error of 0.0046.

the previously cited result from Equation 1: China's GDP is approximately $1,200 billion; hence, a $10 billion reduction in FDI would represent 0.83 percent of GDP, and according to Equation 2 would reduce expected GDP annual growth by (0.83) (1.0046) = 0.0834 percent.

Thus, Equation 1 suggests that a $10 billion reduction in FDI would lower annual GDP growth by 1.6 percent, while Equation 2 suggests a $10 billion reduction in FDI would lower GDP growth by 0.83 percent. If FDI were to shrink by $30 billion, the implied reduction in annual GDP growth might vary between –2.5 percent and –4.8 percent—figures that seem on the face of it to be much too high, so the underlying assumption of linearity is probably faulty.

Another approach to estimating the effects of FDI and its possible shrinkage on China's economic performance is to consider the effects of foreign investment on total factor productivity (TFP) in a standard Solow-Cobb Douglas aggregate production function model, which has been used in other RAND work by the authors.[21] In this prior work, we roughly estimated China's annual rate of growth in TFP to be between 1.0 and 1.5 percent annually. Perhaps, two-thirds of this upper estimate of TFP growth might be attributed to the effects of cumulative FDI flows.[22] From this assumption, we might infer that a substantial shrinkage of FDI, say, perhaps by $10 billion to $20 billion annually might reduce TFP growth by 0.75 percent per year, a rough, subjective estimate that is not widely different from the regression estimates.

A third approach—no less crude than the other two—is to infer from the qualitative survey mentioned earlier an estimate of the effects of possible FDI shrinkage. Combining the survey responses by the proportions expressing them—nearly two-thirds of respondents judged

---

[21]See Wolf et al., 2000, Appendix A, pp. 81–85. See also Edward M. Graham and Erika Wada, "Foreign Direct Investment in China: Effects on Growth and Economic Performance," in Peter Drysdale, ed., *Achieving High Growth: Experience of Transitional Economies in East Asia*, Oxford, 2001. Graham and Wada use the TFP model to estimate differences in growth rates among China's regions and provinces, in accordance with assumptions about their relative inflows of foreign direct investment.

[22]Support for this arguable judgment is provided by the first mechanism cited earlier through which FDI exercises a significant influence on technological progress, see above subsection, Two Mechanisms.

that FDI changes would have "small" effects on GDP growth—suggests that a shrinkage of FDI by, say, 20 percent (i.e., by $10 billion) would reduce annual expected GDP growth by about 0.6 percent.[23]

CONCLUSIONS

Our main conclusions can be summarized as follows:

- Between 1985 and 2001, FDI in China grew from $2.2 billion annually to over $42 billion. In constant 1995 dollars, FDI grew monotonically throughout this period until 1998, experiencing modest declines thereafter through 2001. Averaging over the 16-year period, the compound annual growth rate of FDI was 18.5 percent.

- There are numerous and plausible internal as well as external circumstances that could severely worsen the environment for foreign investment (and, of course, by the same token there are internal as well as external circumstances that could enhance the environment for foreign investment).

- If the adverse circumstances were to occur separately, and more especially if they were to occur collectively or in clusters, they could cause a severe decline in foreign investment.

- In turn, substantial decreases in FDI could have serious negative effects on China's economic performance.

- Our several, admittedly uncertain, estimates suggest that a $10 billion reduction in annual FDI might lower China's annual GDP growth by somewhere between 0.06 and 1.6 percent.

---

[23]Derived by assuming that (a) the judgment of "small" effects of FDI changes can be approximated as 0.025 percent annually (62 percent of respondents), and (b) the judgment of "moderate" effects can be approximated as 0.075 percent annually. Hence, the effects of a $10 billion FDI shrinkage would be $[0.025(0.62) + 0.075(0.38)]/2 = 0.0275/5 \cong 0.0055$.

PART IV

SECURITY FAULT LINES

Chapter Nine

TAIWAN AND OTHER POTENTIAL CONFLICTS

BACKGROUND AND CURRENT STATUS

The current and recent status of relations between the People's Republic of China (PRC) and Taiwan can be characterized as movement without progress. Both China and Taiwan have been admitted to WTO membership. Trade and investment relations between them—mainly conducted indirectly through Hong Kong—continue to flourish, and the tone of occasional rhetorical exchanges between them though rarely warm is not bellicose. These exchanges have been periodically propitiated by official PRC endorsement of bilateral conversations between business groups in Taiwan and mainland China on the subject of direct economic linkages between the two.

The status quo entails benefits for both the PRC and Taiwan, as well as the United States—especially when compared with some of the possible alternatives to it and the paths that might be associated with movement toward these alternatives. Thus, the status quo allows the PRC to concentrate its resources—physical and financial resources, and especially the key resources represented by the time and attention of its new leadership—on the numerous difficult challenges described in the preceding chapters of this study.

Similarly, the status quo enables Taiwan to pursue its overdue efforts to restructure and reform an economy overly dependent on exports and distorted and corrupted by decades of the KMT's (Taiwan's Nationalist Party's) overt and covert penetration of political influence into industry and finance, as well as efforts to enhance and mature its impressively evolving democracy.

The status quo also enables the PRC and Taiwan to accommodate their respective WTO commitments without jeopardizing this process by political or military conflict between them. Furthermore, the status quo has the considerable benefit for both parties of extending the time horizon in which leadership and institutional changes in the PRC may move in political and economic directions that would be more congenial to and compatible with those in Taiwan, thereby facilitating unification, or at least harmony, between them in the longer run.

From the U.S. point of view, the status quo also has major advantages. It enables the United States to pursue its top-priority national security focus on the complex, multifaceted war on terrorism, with at least modest support from both the PRC and Taiwan, and without the serious distraction that a possible crisis in the Taiwan Strait would create.

However, the status quo also entails consequential risks for the parties—risks that may lead to destabilizing moves by them with serious consequences. For example, from the PRC's standpoint, continuance of the status quo, including Taiwan's admission to the WTO as a customs entity, may further enhance Taiwan's *de facto* stature as an independent state. For Taiwan, continuation of the status quo entails a possibly increased risk of its being "encircled," isolated, or even shunted into irrelevance by China's plausible ascent to a dominant economic, political, and military position in the Asian region. Among the indicators of this possibility are the following:

- Expressions of concern by Taiwan's top leadership that it faces "growing business pressure" (from Taiwan as well as U.S. and other foreign business interests) to establish the "three links"—trade, aviation, and postal service—between Taiwan and the mainland.

- Increasing advocacy by some Asian governments and academics of movement toward an Association of Southeast Asian Nations (ASEAN)-China Free Trade Zone, along with the possible future establishment of the Chinese RMB as a zonal currency for the trade zone.

THE POSSIBILITY OF SERIOUS DETERIORATION FROM THE STATUS QUO

One of the major adversities that could derail China's sustained economic growth is a possible deterioration of the status quo from relative quiescence to tension, hostility, and military conflict. The deterioration might escalate from a blockade to a missile attack from the mainland, and even to invasion.

Security analysts in Taiwan envisage scenarios at the second and third rungs of this escalation ladder as plausible possibilities. They envisage that the PRC might "launch a series of missile strikes to damage or destroy" Taiwan's air bases, runways, radar stations, and port facilities, "to enable the PLA [People's Liberation Army] air force and navy to secure air and sea control in the Taiwan Strait" and to create a "tremendous psychological impact on civilians [that] could compromise Taiwan's emergency mobilization and morale."[1] Some Taiwan security analysts suggest that China's 150-plus ballistic missiles would be able to accomplish these results and thereby pave the way for special forces and rapid reaction forces from the mainland to invade and physically occupy, control, and "reunify" Taiwan with the mainland.

While this scenario is not entirely unrealistic, there are numerous technical and logistic reasons for skepticism about its practicability. Furthermore, this scenario would appear to be a distinctly less favored option were the PRC's leadership to decide to use coercive force to resolve the Taiwan issue.[2] One major reason why such an escalatory strategy would be less favored is that its outcome might be precariously ambivalent, conceivably even resulting in a loss by the PRC, thereby seriously damaging the leadership's stature and the legitimacy of the PRC regime. Among the factors that could lead to this outcome are Taiwan's recent and prospective military en-

---

[1]Andrew Yang, *Cross-Strait Arms Competition and Impact on East Asia Security*, Asia-Pacific Center for Security Studies Conference on "Conventional Arms Rivalry in the Asia Pacific," Honolulu, Hawaii, October 2001.

[2]See David Shlapak, David T. Orletsky, and Barry Wilson, *Dire Strait? Military Aspects of the China-Taiwan Confrontation and Options for U.S. Policy*, RAND, Santa Monica, Calif., MR-1217-SRF, 2000.

hancements from U.S. weapons sales, including F-16s, AEGIS missile defense, and diesel submarines.[3]

Instead, a more plausible scenario for use of coercive force by the PRC to accomplish its reunification objective is one that RAND developed for a political-military-economic war game conducted for Taiwan's National Security Council in 1999. Although this scenario would confront the PRC with possible U.S. intervention, the likelihood of intervention would perhaps be diminished because the challenge would be more ambiguous than in the scenario previously described.

In the scenario that we believe is more plausible, the precipitating circumstances and responses to them would be more gradual and ambiguous. Consider the following sequence of events. The PRC might become increasingly frustrated and antagonized by Taiwan's accumulating success in enhancing its international stature through diplomatic initiatives, military modernization, international economic cooperation, and its own national economic performance. Reflecting the PRC's repeated and unheeded expressions of concern and aggravation about these affronts to its sovereignty, the PRC might, in this scenario, be moved to deliver a definitive warning to Taiwan expressing Taiwan's obligation to rescind these hostile moves, or face serious consequences.

If, as would be likely, Taiwan refused to accede to these demands, instead calling them threatening and confrontational, the PRC might plausibly declare a blockade of Taiwan's two principal ports, Kaoshiung and Keelong. Such a blockade could be enforced by perhaps a dozen initial missile launchings in areas adjacent to the sea lines of communications (SLOCs) approaching these ports. The PRC might then formally declare that merchant ships entering these SLOCs would be subject to the risk of attack unless they were to reverse course upon receiving warning from Beijing.

---

[3]Indicative of this possibility is the recent purchase by a unit of U.S. Bank One of a 75 percent controlling stake in a German submarine producer; prior to this acquisition, it was unclear whether and how the United States could include diesel submarines in its possible sales to Taiwan because of a lack of production facilities for making them. See WSJ, June 13, 2002. See also Yang, 2001, op. cit., pp. 7–9.

Taiwan's economy would be extremely vulnerable to such a blockade. Its foreign trade is about 75 percent as large as its GDP, and 95 percent of Taiwan's energy consumption is imported. Of the total volume of its sea traffic, about 30 percent is carried by Taiwan's own merchant fleet, an additional 20 percent by "convenient-flag" vessels registered in other countries by Taiwanese firms, and more than 50 percent of the traffic is carried by ships of other countries. The latter would, very likely, be especially sensitive to and probably deterred by the PRC's blockade. Insurance premiums for commerce in the Taiwan Strait would drastically rise. In the wake of these events, a near-panic wave of stock market selling might ensue in Taiwan. The Taipei stock index could well plummet within a few days by 30 or 40 percent (say, from 5,400 to 3,000), the Taiwan yuan might depreciate sharply from, say, 34 per U.S. dollar to 40–45—the lowest value in the past decade.

While there would be significant repercussions on the mainland in the Shanghai and Shenzhen stock markets, these repercussions would likely be less severe—perhaps reducing market capitalizations by 15–20 percent, rather than 30–40 percent. However, foreign direct investment and foreign portfolio investment in China would likely cease completely in the short- to mid-term.

Under these circumstances, the key question that would arise pertains to the U.S. reaction, as well as anticipation of this reaction by the PRC. U.S. reaction is not a foregone conclusion. Were the United States to be deeply immersed in Operation Enduring Freedom (the Pentagon's umbrella label for the global war against terrorism)—perhaps along with reaffirmation by the PRC of its support for that effort—and were the circumstances surrounding this scenario sufficiently shrouded in ambiguity, and were the United States perhaps to be further distracted by such other events as proliferation of weapons of mass destruction to one or more terrorist organizations with the support of one or more of the "axis-of-evil" powers, then the United States might plausibly be expected to avoid committing forces to support Taiwan.

However this sequence of events might develop, and indeed in advance of its occurrence, the growth of tensions between the PRC and Taiwan would have serious effects on the economies of both China and Taiwan. RAND's most recent forecasts of China's economic growth between 2000 and 2005 placed its average annual rate at about 5 percent. Associated with this growth, we estimated China's military spending in 2005 to be $31–$46 billion in 1998 U.S. dollars at nominal exchange rates and $152–$228 billion in 1998 U.S. dollars at purchasing power parity rates of exchange, with China's accumulation of military capital placed at $84–$106 billion at nominal exchange rates and $295–$374 billion in purchasing power parity rates.[4]

Since these estimates were made in 2000, China's military spending has increased more rapidly—approximately 14 percent in real terms per annum—than our estimates envisaged. Under the circumstances assumed in the scenario outlined above, it would not be unreasonable to anticipate that ensuing reallocations from other uses (and especially for meeting other resource claims arising from the various types of adversities described in the preceding chapters of this study) would further boost China's military spending by perhaps an additional 10 to 20 percent. As a further consequence, the rate of growth in the civil capital stock posited in our previous estimates might fall from 8 to 9 percent annually by as much as 2 percentage points to a lower annual figure, between 6 and 7 percent, while the average annual rate of growth in total factor productivity would plausibly decline by, say, 0.5 percent.[5]

The result of these reallocations can plausibly be estimated as reducing China's rate of economic growth by between 1.0 and 1.3 percent per year.[6] In addition, it can be plausibly inferred that foreign direct investment would severely shrink, not simply in the short run during the crisis in the Taiwan Strait, but for a lengthy period. This would result from a combination of increased allowance for risks, from higher costs of cargo insurance, from exchange rate uncertainties, and from reduced means and increased costs of hedging these risks.

---

[4]See Wolf et al., 2000.

[5]See ibid., pp. 34–36 and pp. 88–89. See also Figure 1.1 in the above chapter showing the interactions referred to in this text.

[6]This rough estimate is derived by applying the capital share (0.4) in GDP to the assumed reduction in the growth of capital stock, plus the assumed reduction in TFP: Reduction in GDP growth = (0.4)(0.02) + (0.005) = 1.3 percent.

This chain of circumstances is what we referred to earlier[7] as China's risk-adjusted, after-tax return on investment, compared with that in other emerging markets and in capital-exporting countries themselves. Investing in China would become less attractive for foreign investors compared with investing elsewhere.

The ensuing impact on the Taiwan economy would be even more grievous, despite the considerable efforts that Taiwan has been making both to upgrade its defensive capabilities against missile attack on the island and against its SLOCs. These efforts and their associated expenditures involve effective early-warning radar systems to detect multiple missile threats over the horizon and acquiring land-based and sea-based missile defense systems and integrating them through better battle management and command and control systems. Taiwan's "defensive" efforts also include measures to acquire offensive capabilities against the mainland (including the submarine assets referred to earlier) for deterrent as well as warfighting purposes.

However well those military enhancements proceed, they would hardly spare the Taiwan economy from deeply adverse consequences. Taipei's plans for economic restructuring would be indefinitely postponed; Taiwan's domestic capital markets and Taiwan's access to foreign direct and portfolio investment would be gravely undermined, and its socioeconomic outlook would sharply deteriorate.

OTHER CONFLICT POSSIBILITIES

While the Taiwan Strait is certainly the "wildest" card among conflict adversities facing China, there are several other "untamed" cards, as well. Although less grave, they would have unsettling repercussions throughout the region and, more specifically, negative effects on China's economic growth prospects.

There are four lower-level conflict contingencies that might involve China, as well as have serious consequences on it. Briefly summarized, they are as follows:

---

[7]See above, Chapter Eight, pp. 149 ff.

- Recurring and intensified *frictions in the South China Sea* over the issue of the PRC's sovereignty claims relating to oil exploration and exploitation in the South China Sea, and the extent of its claimed maritime waters. According to PRC claims, China's riparian rights extend 200 miles from any abutting island that is a part of China. China's claims are contested by Malaysia, the Philippines, Indonesia, and Vietnam, which contend that the riparian rights are limited to 12 miles from the nearest island claimed by China. Were China to attempt to enforce these claims by using its expanding naval capabilities, or to prevent the exercise of counterclaims by one or more of the Southeast Asian countries, adverse effects would ensue with respect to China's internal development, and especially with respect to its ability to attract foreign investment. These adverse effects would be consequential, though of smaller scale than those associated with a security crisis over Taiwan.

- As Chinese naval capabilities expand, periodic disputes in the past might recur between China and Japan over the *Senkaku/Diaoyu islands*, which are claimed by both countries. If, as seems not unlikely, Japan's own considerable naval capabilities were to contest and repel China's assertions of sovereignty over these islands, a serious confrontation between them could ensue.

Also, it is not implausible that political developments in Japan may be moving in the direction of a strengthening of relatively hard-line, antipiracy, and expanded naval and air force military capabilities. These developments might make a confrontation between China and Japan more likely in the future than it has been in the past.

Were such a confrontation to ensue, and once again reverting to Figure 1.1 in Chapter One, the ensuing heightened resource claims for military spending and military procurement in China would have consequential effects on slower rates of civilian capital formation and reduced total factor productivity, thereby lowering China's expected growth rates.[8]

---

[8]See above p. 164.

- Another contingency is one that might arise on the *Korean peninsula*. Were North and South Korea to become engaged in conflict—one that presumably would have been initiated or provoked by the north—China might be inclined, if not compelled, to support its communist neighbor. However the contingency might evolve, its effect on the allocation of China's domestic resources, and quite possibly on the further upward adjustment in expected rates of return required by foreign investors to allow for the added risks they would face, would have severely adverse consequences for China's economic growth.

- Finally, tensions between *China and India* might grow if, for example, the PRC's military and technical assistance to Pakistan were, or at least perceived by India, to add fuel to the Kashmir fires that India has attempted to extinguish. The result could be a resumption of the Sino-Indian border clashes of the mid-1970s and early 1980s, with possible further escalation beyond those prior clashes. Once again, the consequences for reallocation of resources in China—perhaps reducing rates of civil capital formation as well as of factor productivity growth—would have negative effects on China's prospective economic growth.

The bottom line of this summary of conflict contingencies that China may face in the coming years is simple: They constitute another of the numerous and serious obstacles and potential adversities that China confronts in its efforts to sustain high rates of economic modernization and expansion in the coming decades.

Chapter Ten

CONCLUSIONS: FAULT LINES IN CHINA'S ECONOMIC TERRAIN

As indicated in Chapter One, the focus of this research has been on the potential adversities or fault lines facing China's economy and affecting its prospects for sustaining high growth through the coming decade. Thus, we have deliberately concentrated on what might go seriously awry in the economy and, in the process, slow or even reverse China's double-digit growth rates in the 1980s and high single-digit growth in the 1990s and the early part of the 21st century.

We have not devoted equivalent attention to the other side of this coin—the policies and resource reallocations China might devise to prevent, mitigate, or remedy the adversities that otherwise would hinder or reverse its economic growth.

This asymmetry is deliberate. Its intent is to provide a countervailing perspective to what has been a generally prevailing consensus—with a few notable exceptions—among policymakers, businessmen, and scholars both within and outside China: namely, that China's economy will be able to sustain high rates of economic growth for the indefinite future. This consensus is, for example, reflected in analyses and forecasts by the World Bank, the OECD, the Institute for International Economics, and in the hearings and final report of the U.S.-China Security Review Commission.[1]

---

[1] See reference reports, memoranda, and other papers published by these organizations.

In considering what might go seriously wrong in the Chinese economy, we have focused on eight domains, described in Chapters Two–Nine. For each of them, we have tried to arrive at a bottom line in terms of their respective effects on China's annual growth rate, should each of these adversities occur. To arrive at each bottom line, we have used either the aggregate growth model employed in other RAND work on the Chinese and other Asian economies,[2] or specific calculations tailored to and described in each of the eight separate chapters.

FINDINGS AND BOTTOM LINES

Our principal findings together with our estimates about the corresponding bottom lines can be summarized as follows.

Unemployment, Poverty, and Social Unrest

Open and disguised unemployment in China totals about 170 million, or about 23 percent of the total labor force in 1999. Moreover, the level of unemployment has been rising due especially to the population increase in the 1980s, as well as to the privatization of SOEs in the 1990s along with the downsizing of these often inefficient, loss-incurring enterprises. Recent and prospective increases in unemployment have not been principally the result of China's efforts to comply with its WTO commitments, although these commitments may engender further unemployment. The aggregate statistics have been accompanied by rising urban unemployment resulting *from* rural poverty, and resulting *in* income inequality between rural and urban areas, rural-to-urban migration, and social unrest.

The *bottom line* in this domain is our estimate of lower total factor productivity, lower savings, and reduced capital formation, causing reductions between 0.3 and 0.8 percent in China's annual growth rate over the next decade.

---

[2]See Wolf et al., 2000.

Economic Effects of Corruption

Both the concept and the measurement of corruption are complex as well as more than slightly obscure. Corruption in China as elsewhere includes the circumvention of established rules and laws. But some rules and laws in China as elsewhere may be perverse with respect to economic growth so their evasion may help rather than hinder growth.

In our effort to calibrate corruption in China and to link a possible adverse change in corrupt practices to their impact on China's expected economic performance, we have drawn on two established indices of corruption. These indices are based on polls, questionnaires, and surveys and include such categories as legal structure and security of property rights, regulation of business, and "perceptions" of corruption. In turn, the quintiles of the corruption indices are associated with differing quintile positions in annual economic growth rates of various countries included in the relevant indices. We infer that, were corrupt practices in China to increase—thereby lowering the quintile position of China in terms of its associated economic growth—our crude *bottom-line* estimate of the impact on China's expected growth rate would be a reduction of about 0.5 percent.

A recent estimate by Angang Hu has placed the economic cost of corruption in China in a range between 13.2 and 16.8 percent of GDP in the mid- to late 1990s.[3] However, this estimate seems to us to be too high for technical reasons discussed in Chapter Three. Moreover, the aggregate estimate of 13.2 refers to the *level* of economic cost imposed on the system, rather than the effect of a change in this level on China's growth.

HIV/AIDS and Epidemic Disease

Estimates by the United Nations and other sources have placed the prevalence of HIV/AIDS in China in a range between 600,000 and 1.3 million, with an approximate annual rate of increase between 20 and 30 percent. For the several health scenarios analyzed in this study, estimated HIV carriers in the second decade of this century could

---

[3]Angang Hu, 2002, op. cit.

range between 11 million and 80 million in China. By 2015, China's HIV population would exceed the entire HIV population of sub-Saharan Africa today!

One way of translating these prevalence estimates into economic burdens is to consider the costs of treatment. At a minimum level, based on India's experience, annual treatment costs are $600 per person.

If, for example, the prospectively infected population in China is between 5 and 10 million, the costs of treatment would be $3–6 billion a year at a minimum, and rising. Based on the "intermediate," rather than "pessimistic" scenario described in Chapter Four, China's population would experience annual deaths from HIV/AIDS between 1.7 and 2.7 million in the second decade of the 21st century, cumulating by 2025 to over 20 million casualties, associated with health-based reductions in productivity and annual reductions in GDP growth between 1.8 and 2.2 percent in the period 2002–2015.

Water Resources and Pollution

Although China's aggregate water supplies are adequate, China is beset by a perennial maldistribution of natural water supplies. The North China plain, with over a third of China's total population and at least an equivalent share of its GDP, has only 7.5 percent of the naturally available water resources. Subsurface aquifers in North China are near exhaustion, and pollution discharges from industrial and other uses further aggravate the shortage of water available for consumers and industry. By contrast, South China normally has an abundance of natural water supplies, sometimes leading to floods. The dilemma this poses for China's policymakers is whether and to what extent to push for capital-intensive water-transfer projects from south to north or, instead, to emphasize recycling as well as conservation of restricted water supplies in the north, or to pursue some combination of these alternatives.

This key allocation issue is further complicated by political considerations relating to the relative influence of provinces in the north and south regions. Our analysis in Chapter Five examines several different scenarios involving different combinations of water-transfer projects and recycling/conservation efforts which, in general, are more efficient from the standpoint of reducing the short- to medium-term stringencies in water resource availability in the north. If, for various reasons, nonoptimal policy decisions and resource allocations are pursued, a plausible "pessimistic" scenario could result in reducing China's annual GDP growth between 1.5 and 1.9 percent.

Energy Consumption and Prices

The risk posed for China's continued high growth rate by availability of oil and natural gas supplies arises from the possibility of major increases in world energy prices, rather than from the fact that China has shifted from being a net exporter of oil in the early 1990s to a current and future situation in which nearly half of its oil and nearly a fifth of its natural gas consumption are derived from imports.

To analyze the fault line that might arise in the energy sector, we posit a scenario in which there is a drastic contraction in global oil supply, for whatever reason or combination of reasons, by about 25 percent and lasting for a decade (2005–2015). Factoring into this scenario a range of plausible demand elasticities, together with a small allowance for increased energy efficiency, we conservatively infer that global oil prices might rise as much as threefold. The resulting effect on China's annual growth rate resulting from a "moderately severe" scenario during the period 2005–2015 would be an average diminution between 1.2 and 1.4 percent.

China's Fragile Financial System and State-Owned Enterprises

One of the salient indicators of systemic fragility of China's state-dominated financial institutions is the extraordinarily high ratio of nonperforming loans on the balance sheets of the four major state banks. These NPLs have risen and continue to rise as the result of accumulated "policy lending" from the state banks to loss-incurring SOEs. Estimates of total NPLs cover an enormous range, between 9 and 60 percent of China's GDP. The correct figure is more likely to be at the upper end of this range.

Under circumstances that are discussed in Chapter Seven, China could experience a "run" of withdrawals from the state banks, large-scale capital flight, a significant reduction in savings rates, and a decline of capital formation. The resulting financial crisis and credit squeeze could plausibly reduce total factor productivity by 0.3 percent, with accompanying reductions in the rates of capital formation and of employment growth that would collectively lower annual GDP growth by 0.5 to 1.0 percent.

Possible Shrinkage of Foreign Direct Investment

Between 1985 and 2001, the annual compound rate of growth in foreign direct investment in China was over 18 percent, rising from an annual rate of about $2 billion to over $40 billion in 2001 (in constant 1995 dollars). Two different mechanisms discussed in Chapter Eight are generally believed to account for the special importance and leveraging effects of foreign direct investment in contributing to China's high growth rates during the 1985–2001 period.

Yet there are not implausible circumstances under which this pattern of secularly rising FDI might severely contract. These adverse circumstances include both possible *internal* developments (such as tensions accompanying the leadership succession, internal financial crisis, inconvertibility of the RMB, repercussions from a possible HIV/AIDS epidemic, and slow implementation of China's WTO pledges), as well as possible *external* developments (such as improvements in the economic infrastructure and investment climate in other competing countries and regions in Eastern Europe, Russia, India, and elsewhere). To a greater extent than has occurred in the past, future FDI in China is likely to depend critically on the *comparative* risk-adjusted, after-tax return on investment in China compared with that in other countries.

Based on several rough assumptions and crude calculations, a sustained reduction of $10 billion a year in FDI may be associated with a reduction of China's annual GDP growth between 0.8 and 1.6 percent.

Taiwan and Other Potential Conflicts

The current and recent status of relations between China and Taiwan is characterized in Chapter Nine as "movement without progress."

Yet this status quo entails major benefits for the PRC and Taiwan, as well as for the United States, especially when compared with some of the possible alternatives to it and the paths that might be associated with movement toward them.

There are also significant risks and tensions associated with the status quo, and it is not implausible that these might erupt into possible conflict between the PRC and Taiwan. In Chapter Nine, we consider one scenario involving escalation from provocation by Taiwan as viewed from Beijing, a blockade imposed in response, tangible though limited coercive force to effectuate the blockade, and the resulting effects on China's reallocation of resources to military spending, with ensuing reductions in the rate of growth of the civil capital stock and in the growth of total factor productivity.

The *bottom line* of these adverse security developments would be a conservative estimate of a decline in China's annual rate of economic growth between 1.0 and 1.3 percent.

SUMMARY

Table 10.1 summarizes our rough estimates of the plausible impacts on China's annual growth that could ensue from each of the adversities or fault lines that we have considered separately from one another. As noted earlier, five of these are already present and, in these instances, what we are positing is the possibility of their becoming worse and the economic effects this would entail.

As is evident in Table 10.1, and in the preceding subsections of this chapter, sustaining China's high growth from the past into the period 2003–2010 faces major obstacles, challenges, and what we have called "adversities." These include the several categories of adversities—sectoral, institutional, financial, and security—that we have analyzed in the successive chapters of this study.

The probability that none of these individual adversities will occur is low, while the probability that *all* will ensue is still lower. Were all of the setbacks to occur, the effect, according to our estimates, would be growth reductions of 7.4–10.7 percent; thus, improbably registering negative numbers for China's economic performance. While the probability that all of these adversities will occur is low, the probability that several will occur is higher than their simple joint, multiplicative probabilities would normally imply. The reason for this multiplication is that their individual probabilities are not independent of one another. Several of the separate adversities may tend to cluster because of these interdependencies. For example, an internal financial crisis would have serious negative consequences for the relative attractiveness of foreign investment in China and would be conducive to shrinkage of FDI. Similarly, tension or conflict in the Taiwan Straight or in other parts of the Asia-Pacific region would very likely seriously diminish FDI in China, as well as increase the likelihood of a financial crisis. Another clustering might arise in connection with the interdependence among unemployment, poverty, and the incidence of epidemic disease, including HIV/AIDS.

Table 10.2 suggests some of the key interdependencies among the several fault lines we have discussed.

Table 10.1

Impacts on China's Growth Arising from Separate Fault Lines, 2005–2015 (Preliminary)

Type of Setback	Separate Effects Diminishing China's Economic Performance (percentage/year)
Unemployment, poverty, social unrest	0.3–0.8
Economic effects of corruption	0.5
HIV/AIDS and epidemic disease	1.8–2.2
Water resources and pollution	1.5–1.9
Energy consumption and prices	1.2–1.4
Fragility of the financial system and state-owned enterprises	0.5–1.0
Possible shrinkage of foreign direct investment	0.6–1.6
Taiwan and other potential conflicts	1.0–1.3

Table 10.2

Interdependencies Among Fault Lines

Consequence	Cause							
	Unemployment, poverty, and social unrest	Economic effects of corruption	HIV/AIDS and epidemic disease	Water resources and pollution	Energy consumption and prices	Fragility of the financial system and state-owned enterprises	Possible shrinkage of foreign direct investment	Taiwan and other potential conflicts
Unemployment, poverty, and social unrest		✔	✔	✔	✔	✔		
Economic effects of corruption	✔					✔	✔	
HIV/AIDS and epidemic disease	✔			✔	✔			
Water resources and pollution	✔		✔		✔			
Energy consumption and prices	✔							
Fragility of the financial system and state-owned enterprises	✔	✔	✔				✔	✔
Possible shrinkage of foreign direct investment	✔	✔	✔			✔		✔
Taiwan and other potential conflicts								

NOTE: ✔ indicates where a fault line (cause/column heading) is likely to affect the occurrence and/or severity of another (consequence/row heading).

EPILOGUE

As noted in Chapter One there are many important questions about China's future. In this study, we have considered only one of them. What are the major challenges, fault lines, and potential adversities that confront China in its efforts to sustain a high rate of economic growth in the coming decades? Our analysis of these fault lines underscores their scale and complexity, and it also suggests that their ramifications will extend into all levels of China's society, government, and party structure.

An important but debatable proposition can be inferred from this analysis: To mitigate the stresses engendered by these fault lines will demand an enormous and continuing array of consultations, negotiations, and transactions among China's central and provincial governments and the Communist Party apparatus. This demanding process is likely to preoccupy China's new collective leadership during the next decade, predisposing it to avoid external distractions and to maintain equable relations with the United States.

Alesina, Alberto. 1988. "Macroeconomics and Politics," *NBER Macroeconomics Annual 1988*, MIT Press, Cambridge, Mass.

Almanac. 2001. See China Finance Association.

Barro, Robert J. 1998. Determinants of Economic Growth, MIT Press, Cambridge, Mass.

Bhaduri, A. 1989. "Disguised Unemployment," in J. Eatwell, M. Milgate, and P. Newman, eds., *Economic Development*, W. W. Norton, New York.

Brandon, C., and R. Ramankutty. 1993. *Toward an Environmental Strategy for Asia*, World Bank, Washington, D.C.

Brown, L., and B. Halweil. 1998. "China's Water Shortage Could Shake World Food Security," *World Watch*, Vol. 11, No. 4, July/August, pp. 10–21.

Brown, Lester. 2000. "Falling Water Tables in China May Soon Raise Food Prices Everywhere," *Chairman of the Board Worldwatch Issue Alert*, Earth Policy Institute, www.worldwatch.org/chairman/issue/000502.html.

Buck, J. Lossing. 1964. *Land Utilization in China*, Paragon, New York.

Calvo, Guillermo A., and Jacob A. Frenkel. 1991. "Credit Markets, Credibility, and Economic Transformation," *Journal of Economic Perspectives*, Vol. 5, No. 4, Fall, pp. 139–148.

Caprio, Gerald, and Ross Levine. 1994. "Reforming Finance in Transitional Socialist Economies," *World Bank Research Observer*, Vol. 9, No. 1, pp. 1–24.

CAS. 1998. *Jiaoye yu fazhan* (Employment and Development), Liaoning People's Press, Shanyang.

Chen Naisheng. 1999. "The Interconnection of Economic Development and the Re-Employment Project," *Jingji wenti* (Economic Problems), No. 2, pp. 8–11.

Chen Yuan, ed. 1994. *Zhongguo jinrong tizhi gaige* (Reform of China's Financial System), China Public Finance and Economics Press, Beijing.

Cheng Hang-sheng. 1999. *Can China Achieve Bank Marketization Without Bank Privatization?* The 1990 Institute, San Francisco.

China Daily. 2000. "Nation Warns of Water Scarcity," *China Daily*, March 23.

China Daily. 2001a. "Beijing Works to Provide Cleaner Water," *China Daily*, April 9.

China Daily. 2001b. "Capital to Impose Quota to Save Water," *China Daily*, November 20.

China Daily. 2001c. "China Enhances Flood Control Ability over Major Rivers," *China Daily*, December 21.

China Daily. 2001d. "Diversion to Relieve Drought," *China Daily*, October 31.

China Daily. 2001e. "Grain Security Firmly Anchored," *China Daily*, March 1.

China Daily. 2001f. "Major Cities Take Steps to Protect Water Resources," *China Daily*, March 23.

China Daily. 2001g. "State Set to Begin Ambitious Yangtze Diversion Project," *China Daily*, November 15, 2001.

China Daily. 2001h. "Water Projects to Add Business to Life," *China Daily*, December 4.

China Daily. 2002. "Rice Cropped for Water," *China Daily,* January 9.

China Finance Association. 2001. *Zhongguo jinrong nianjian 2001* (Almanac of China's Finance and Banking, 2001), China Financial Yearbook Editorial Department, Beijing. Hereafter referred to as Almanac, 2001.

China Labor Association. 1992. *Shijimmo de tiaozhan* (Challenge at the Turn of the Century), China Labor Press, Beijing.

Chow, Gregory C. 1994. *Understanding China's Economy,* World Scientific, Singapore.

Cook, Sarah. 1999. "Surplus Labor and Productivity in Chinese Agriculture: Evidence from Household Survey Data," *Journal of Development Studies,* Vol. 35, No. 3, February, pp. 16–44.

Cukierman, Alex. 1992. "Dynamics of Optimal Gradual Stabilization," *World Bank Economic Review,* No. 6, September, pp. 439–458.

Dai Xianglong, ed. 1997. *Lingdao ganpu jinrong zhixi dupen* (Textbook on Financial Knowledge for Leading Cadres), China Finance Press, Beijing.

Dai Xianglong and Gui Xiyong, eds. 1997. *Zhongguo jinrong gaige yu fazhan* (Reform and Development of China's Finance), China Finance Press, Beijing.

Dasgupta, Susmita, Mainul Huq, David Wheeler, and Chonghua Zhang. 2001. "Water Pollution Abatement by Chinese Industry: Cost Estimates and Policy Implications," *Applied Econometrics,* Vol. 33, pp. 547–557. (Reprint of World Bank Policy Research Working Paper No. 1630 in 1996.)

Deng Xiaoping. 1993. *Deng Xiaoping wenxuan* (Selected Works of Deng Xiaoping), Vol. III, People's Press, Beijing.

Deng Yingtao, Xu Xiaobo, et al. 1994. *Zhongguo nongcun jinrong de biange yu fazhan 1978–1990* (Changes and Development in China's Rural Finance, 1978–1990), Oxford University Press, Hong Kong.

Development Research Center (DRC), State Council. 1994. *Jingji fazhan gaige yu zhentse* (Economic Development, Reform, and Policies), Social Science Document Press, Beijing.

Dong, Furen. 1994. *Jingji tizhi gaige yanjiu* (Studies in Economic System Reform), Economic Science Press, Beijing.

Economic Review. 1992. No. 6, September, pp. 439–458.

"Economic Transformation." 1991. *Journal of Economic Perspectives*, Vol. 5, No. 4.

Economy, E. 1997. *Reforms and Resources: The Implication for State Capacity in the PRC,* www.library.utoronto.ca/www/pcs/state/china/china1.htm.

Fan Moyong and Hou Hongxiang. 2000. "An Analysis of China's Hidden Rural Unemployment," *Jingji wenti* (Economic Problems), No. 6, pp. 6–9.

Fazhan 1978–1990.

Feilig, Gerhard K. 1999. *Can China Feed Itself? A System for Evaluation of Policy Options,* International Institute for Applied Systems Analysis, Laxenburg, Austria.

Feng Lanrui. 1992. "Comparative Studies of the Two Unemployment Peaks in the Past Ten Years," *Jingji shehui tizhi bijiao* (Comparison of Socioeconomic Systems), No. 5, September 20, pp. 37–42.

Grille, V., D. Masciandaro, and G. Tabellini. 1991. "Political and Monetary Institutions, and Public Finance Policies in the Industrial Countries," *Economic Policy,* No. 13, October, pp. 341–392.

Hainan. 1992. *Zhongguo: Zhongyang yinhang yu zhipan xichang* (China: Central Bank and Capital Markets), China (Hainan) Reform Development Research Institute.

Holz, Carsten. 1992. *The Role of Central Banking in China's Economic Reforms*, East Asia Program, Cornell University, Ithaca, New York.

Holz, Carsten, and Tian Zhu. 2000. "Banking and Enterprise Reform in the People's Republic of China After the Asian Financial Crisis: An Appraisal," *Asian Development Review*, Vol. 18, No. 1, pp. 73–91.

Hsu, Hsin-Hui, and Fred Gale. 2001. *China: Agriculture in Transition.* ERS Agriculture and Trade Report No. 012, Beijing, November.

Hu Angang. 2000. *Zhongguo zhoxiang* (Prospects of China), Zhejiang People's Press, Hangzhou.

Hu Angang. 2001a. "China's Present Economic Situation and Its Macro-Economic Policies," Paper presented at RAND-China Reform Forum Conference, Santa Monica, November 29–30, 2001.

Hu Angang. 2001b. *Creative Destruction of Restructuring: China's Urban Unemployment and Social Security* (mimeograph).

Huang, Jikun, Scott Rozelle, and Linxiu Zhang. 2000. "WTO and Agriculture: Radical Reforms or the Continuation of Gradual Transition," *China Economic Review,* Vol. 11, pp. 397–401.

International Labor Office. 1970. *Towards Full Employment,* Geneva.

Johnson, D. Gale. 2000. "The WTO and Agriculture in China," *China Economic Review,* Vol. 11, pp. 402–404.

Kao, C.H.C., K. R. Anschel, and C. K. Eicher. 1964. "Disguised Unemployment in Agriculture: A Survey," in C. Eicher and L. Witt, eds., *Agriculture in Economic Development,* McGraw-Hill, New York, pp. 129–144.

Kindleberger, Charles P., and Bruce Herrick. 1977. *Economic Development,* Third Edition, McGraw-Hill, New York.

Kriner, Stephanie. 1999. "Is China Dammed for a Great Flood?" *Disaster Relief,* June 4, www.disasterrelief.org/Disasters/9906023gorges.

Lardy, R. Nicholas. 1998. *China's Unfinished Economic Revolution,* Brookings Institute Press, Washington, D.C.

Lee, Sungho. 1998. *Hydrological Metabolism and Water Resources Management of the Beijing Metropolitan Region in the Hai River Basin,* Master of Arts thesis in Geography, University of Toronto.

Lee, Sungho. 2000. *Water Resources Management Planning for the Sustainable Development of Beijing,* Master of Arts thesis in International Relations, International University of Japan.

Li Chengrui. 1959. *Zhongguo renmin kongheguo nongyeshiu shihgao* (A Draft History of Agricultural Tax in People's Republic of China), Public Finance Press, Beijing.

Li Jingwen, ed. 1998. *21 sichi zhong quo jingji da qu* (General Trends in China's Economic Development in the 21st Century), Liaoning People's Press, Shenyang.

Li Qiang, Hu Jinxeng, and Hong Dayung. 2001. *Xiye xiagang wenti duibi yanjiu* (A Comparative Study of the Problem of Unemployment and Deactivated Workers), Qinghua University Press, Beijing.

Lin Fude and Zhai Zhenwu, eds. 1996. *Zhoxiang erhshiyi shiji de zhongguo renkou, huanjing yu fazhan* (China's Population, Environment, and Development Toward the Twenty-First Century), Higher Education Press, Beijing.

Lin, Justin Yifu. 2000. "WTO Accession and China's Agriculture," *China Economic Review*, Vol. 11, pp. 405–408.

Lin Qingsong and Du Ying. 1997. *Zhongguo kongye gaige yu xiaolu* (China's Industrial Reform and Efficiency), Yunnan People's Press, Kunming.

Lin Qingsong. 1995. "An Analysis of the Changes in the Efficiency of China's Industrial Sector Since Reform and Their Underlying Factors," *Jingji yanjiu* (Economic Research), No. 10, pp. 27–34.

Lin Yifu, Hai Wen, and Ping Xinqiao, eds. 2000. *Zhongguo jingji yanjiu* (Studies in Chinese Economy), Beijing University Press, Beijing.

Liu Changming. 1998. Environmental Issues and the South-North Water Transfer Scheme, *The China Quarterly*.

Liu Guoguang, Wang Lolin, and Li Jingwen. 2001. *Zhongguo jingji qianjing fengsi* (An Analysis of China's Economic Prospects), Social Science Documents Press, Beijing.

Liu Jichun, Xu Sulin, and Liu Junru, eds. 1999. *Nongmin fudan 200 wen* (200 Questions Concerning the Peasants' Burden), China Social Press, Beijing.

Long, J. Bradford, and Lawrence H. Summers. 1992. "Macroeconomic Policy and Long-Run Growth," *Policies for Long-Run Economic Growth*, Federal Reserve Bank of Kansas City, Kansas City, Kan.

Ma Guochiang, Su Ming, and Shih Aihu. 1994. *Zhongguo nongmin shouru wenti yanjiu* (A Study of the Problems of Peasants' Incomes in China), Guizhou People's Press, Guiyang.

Ma Hong, ed. 1982. *Xiandai zhongguo jingji shidian* (A Compendium of Economic Institutions in Contemporary China), China Social Science Press, Beijing.

Ma Hong and Wang Mongkui, eds. 2002. *Zhongguo fazhan yanjiu* (China Development Studies), China Development Press, Beijing.

Ma Mingjia. 1993. "Why Must Raising Funds from the Society Be Approved by Proper Authorities?" *RMRB*, July 1, p. 2.

MacLeod, Calum. 2001. "China to Build World's Largest Water-Diversion Project," *ChinaOnline News*, November 14.

Mao Zedong. 1977. *Mao Zedong shuanji* (Selected Works of Mao Zedong), Vol. 5, People's Press, Beijing.

Ministry of Agriculture. 1982. *Zhongguo nongye jingji gaiyao* (China's Agricultural Economy: A Summary), Agriculture Press, Beijing.

Ministry of Agriculture. 1990. "A Survey of Peasants' Burdens," *Nongye jingji wneti* (Problems of Agricultural Economy), No. 2, pp. 57–60.

Ministry of Finance. 1992. *Zhongguo caicheng tongji 1950–1991* (China Public Finance Statistics, 1950–1991), Science Press, Beijing.

Myint, H. 1964. *The Economics of the Developing Countries*, Hutchinson, London.

Myrdal, G. 1968. *Asian Drama*, Pantheon, New York.

National Environmental Protection Agency. 1995–1996. *Environmental Yearbook of China* [in Chinese].

Nickum, J. E. 1994. "Beijing's Maturing Socialist Water Economy," in J. E. Nickum and K. W. Easter, eds., *Metropolitan Water Use Conflicts in Asia and the Pacific*, East-West Center, Westview Press, Colo.

Nickum, J. E., and K. W. Easter. 1994. "Alternative Approaches to Urban Water Management," in J. E. Nickum and K. W. Easter, eds.,

Metropolitan Water Use Conflicts in Asia and the Pacific, East-West Center, Westview Press, Colo.

Nurkse, Ragnar. 1953. *Problems of Capital Formation*, Oxford University Press, New York.

Ogaki, Masao, Jonathan Ostry, and Carman M. Rhinhart. 1996. "Saving Behavior in Low and Middle-Income Developing Countries: A Comparison," *IMF Staff Papers,* March, pp. 38–71.

Paarlberg, Robert L. 1997. "Feeding China: A Confident View," *Food Policy,* Vol. 22, No. 3, pp. 269–279.

PBC. 1994. *Zhongguo jiushi niandai de huobi zhentse* (China's Monetary Policy in the 1990s), China Economic Press, Beijing.

PBC. 1999. "Factors Affecting China's National and Household Savings," *Jingji yanjiu* (Economic Research), No. 5, pp. 3–10.

Ren Caifang, Qiu Xiaohua, and Yan Yulong. 1995. "A Study of China's Monetary Policies," *Jingji yanjiu changkow* (References for Economic Research), No. 91, June 11, pp. 2–8.

SA 01. See SSB. 2001.

Sen, Amartya. 1975. *Employment, Technology and Development*, Clarendon Press, Oxford.

Silk, Mitchell, and Simon Black. 2000. "Financing Options for PRC Water Projects," *ChinaBusiness,* July/August.

Song Changqing. 1995. "China's Unemployment Situation and the Reform of Unemployment Statistics," *Jingji yanjiu changkow* (References for Economic Research), No. 108, July 15, pp. 21–26.

SSB. 1960. *Ten Great Years.* Foreign Languages Press, Peking.

SSB. 1985. *Zhongguo gongye jingji tongji zhilian 1949–1984* (Statistics of China's Industrial Economy, 1949–1984), China Statistics Press, Beijing.

SSB. 1987a. *Zhongguo guding zichan touzi tongji zhiliao 1950–1985* (Statistics of China's Fixed Investment, 1950–1985), China Statistics Press, Beijing.

SSB. 1987b. *Zhongguo laodong gongzhi tongji zhiliao 1949–1985* (Statistics of China's Labor and Wages, 1949–1985), China Statistics Press, Beijing.

SSB. 1988. *Zhongguo jianjuye tongji zhilian 1952–1985* (China Construction Statistics, 1952–1985), China Statistics Press, Beijing.

SSB. 1989a. *Fenjin de sishinian 1949–1989* (Forty Years of Strife and Progress 1949–1989), China Statistics Press, Beijing.

SSB. 1989b. *Zhongguo laodong gongzhi tongji zhilian 1978–1987* (Statistics of China's Labor and Wages, 1978–1987), China Statistics Press, Beijing.

SSB. 1997. *Zhongguo nongcun tongji nianjian 1997* (Rural Statistical Yearbook of China, 1997), China Statistics Press, Beijing.

SSB. 1999. *Xin zhongguo wushinian tongji zhiliao hupian* (Comprehensive Statistical Data and Materials on 50 Years of New China), China Statistics Press, Beijing.

SSB. 2000a. *Xin zhongguo wushinian nongye tongji zhiliao* (Agricultural Statistics of New China in the Last 50 Years), China Statistics Press, Beijing.

SSB. 2000b. (SY 00). *Zhongguo tongji nianjian 2000* (China Statistical Yearbook 2000), China Statistics Press, Beijing. (Yearbooks for other years are similarly abbreviated.)

SSB. 2001. (SA 01). *Zhongguo tongji zheyiao 2001* (China Statistical Abstract, 2001), China Statistics Press, Beijing. (Statistical abstracts for other years are similarly abbreviated.)

SSB and MOL. 1997. *Zhongguo laodong tongji nianjian 1997* (China Labor Statistical Yearbook, 1997), China Statistics Press, Beijing.

SSB and MOLS. 2001. *Zhongguo laodong tongji nianjian 2001* (China Labor Statistical Yearbook, 2001), China Statistics Press, Beijing.

Statistical Agency of the PRC. 1994. *Water Use Yearbook of China,* Beijing [in Chinese].

Statistical Agency of the PRC. 1995–1996. *Urban Statistical Yearbook of China,* Beijing [in Chinese].

Statistical Agency of the PRC. 2000 and 2001. *Statistical Yearbook of China*, Beijing [in Chinese].

Stiglitz, Joseph E. 1994. *Wither Socialism?* MIT Press, Cambridge, Mass.

SY 00. See SSB. 2000b.

Tian Hanqing and Sun Lizhao. 1995. "Bad Loans Threaten Profitability of State Banks," *Guanli shihjie* (Management World), No. 6, 1995, pp. 98–105.

Todaro, M. P. 1994. *Economic Development*, Longman, New York.

Tong Daochi. 1999. *The Heart of Economic Reform: China's Banking Reform and State Enterprise Restructuring*, RGSD-149, RAND, Santa Monica.

Turnham, David. 1993. *Employment and Development: A New Review of Evidence*, OECD, Paris.

United Nations Population Division (UNPD). 1994. *Water Resources Management in North China*, Research Center of North China Water Resources, Beijing.

Wang Dongshen, Chen Lijia, and Hou Fuqing. 1995. "Problems of Employment and Policy Measures During the Ninth Five Year Plan Period," *Jingji yanjiu changkow* (References for Economic Research), No. 108, July 15, pp. 2–11.

Wang, Hua, and Somik Lall. 1999. *Valuing Water for Chinese Industries: A Marginal Productivity Assessment,* Policy Research Working Paper 2236, World Bank, Washington, D.C.

Wolf, Charles, et al. 2000. *Asian Economic Trends and Their Security Implications*, MR-1143-OSD/A, RAND, Santa Monica, Appendix Table B.1, pp. 88–89, and Table 7, p. 36.

World Bank. 1992. *China: Strategies for Reducing Poverty in the 1990s*, World Bank, Washington, D.C.

World Bank. 1994. *World Development Report 1994*, World Bank, Washington, D.C.

World Bank. 1996. *The Chinese Economy: Fighting Inflation, Deepening Reforms*, Vol. I, *The Main Report*, World Bank, Washington, D.C.

World Bank. 1997a. *At China's Table: Food Security Options*, World Bank, Washington, D.C.

World Bank. 1997b. *China 2020: Development Challenges in the New Century*, World Bank, Washington, D.C.

World Bank. 1997c. *China Engaged*, World Bank, Washington, D.C.

World Bank. 1997d. *Clear Water, Blue Skies: China's Environment in the New Century*, World Bank, Washington, D.C.

World Bank. 1997e. *Sharing Rising Incomes*, World Bank, Washington, D.C.

World Bank. 1997f. *Staff Appraisal Report: China Wanjiazhai Water Transfer Project*, Report No. 15999-CHA, World Bank, Washington, D.C.

World Bank. 1997g. *World Development Report, 1997*, World Bank, Washington, D.C.

World Bank. 1999. *World Development Report 1999*, World Bank, Washington, D.C.

World Bank. 2000a. *Project Appraisal Document on a Proposed Loan in the Amount of US$74 Million to the People's Republic of China for the Water Conservation Project*, Report No. 19991-CHA, World Bank, Washington, D.C.

World Bank. 2000b. *World Development Indicators 2000*, World Bank, Washington, D.C.

World Bank. 2000c. *World Development Report 2000/2001: Attacking Poverty*, World Bank, Washington, D.C.

World Bank. 2001a. *2001 World Development Indicators*, World Bank, Washington, D.C.

World Bank. 2001b. *Action Agenda for Water Sector Strategy for North China*, World Bank, Washington, D.C., www.chinaonline.com/commentary_analysis/thiswk_comm/010521/c01051860.asp.

World Bank. 2001c. *China: Air, Land, and Water,* World Bank, Washington, D.C.

World Bank. 2001d. *China: Overcoming Rural Poverty,* World Bank, Washington, D.C.

World Bank. 2001e. *Creative Destruction of Restructuring: China's Urban Unemployment and Social Security* (mimeographed).

World Bank Research Observer. 1994. Vol. 9, No. 1, pp. 1–24.

World Resource Institute (WRI), UNEP, UNPD, and World Bank. 1998. *World Resources 1998–99,* World Resource Institute, Washington, D.C.

World Resource Institute (WRI), UNEP, UNPD, and World Bank. 2000. *World Resources 2000–01,* World Resource Institute, Washington, D.C.

Wu Jinglian. 1992. "China's Economic and Financial Reforms," in Wu Jinglian and Wang Haibo, eds., *Jiushi niandai zhongguo jingji de gaige yu fazhan* (China's Economic Reform and Development in the 1990s), Economic Management Press, Beijing.

Wu Jinglian. 1995. "China's Economic and Financial Reforms," in On Kit Tam, ed., *Financial Reform in China*, Routledge, London, pp. 83–103.

Xe Deren. 1999. "The Paradox of State-Owned Enterprise Debt Ratios: The Problem and Its Interpretation," *Jingji yanjiu* (Economic Research), No. 9, pp. 72–79.

Xe Ping. 2000. "China's Financial Reform Faces Challenges," in Hu Angang, ed., *Zhongguo Zhoxian* (Prospects of China), Zhejiang People's Press, Hangzhou.

Xiao Zhoji. 1993. "Accelerate Financial Reform: An Urgent Task for China's Economic Reform," *Yanjiu baokao* (Research Report), No. 3, pp. 1–5.

Xinhua. 2001a. "Beijing to Invest 24 Billion Yuan Solving Water Shortage," *Xinhua,* June 21.

Xinhua. 2001b. "China's Urban Wastewater Treatment Offers Chances for Overseas Business," *Xinhua,* November 29.

Xu Meizheng. 1997. "Causes and Measures to Resolve Problems of Bank-Enterprise Debts," *Guanli shihjie* (Management World), No. 1, pp. 138–144.

Xue Jiaqi. 1986. "On the Economic Environment for Developing Rural Enterprises," *Nongye jingji wenti* (Problems of Agricultural Economy), No. 4, pp. 4–7.

Yang Teqai. 1997. "An Analysis of Rural Collective Economic Organizations' Borrowing from Civilians," *Guanli shihjie* (Management World), No. 6, pp. 145–150.

Yang Xiaoyong. 1995. "Migration of Peasant Workers and China's Rural and Urban Economic Development," *Renkou yu jingji* (Population and Economics), No. 5, pp. 26–32.

Yang Yiyong et al. 1997. *Xiye qongjibo* (Waves of Impact from Unemployment), China Today Press, Beijing.

Yang, Hong, and Alexander Zehnder. 2001. "China's Regional Water Scarcity and Implications for Grain Supply and Trade," *Environment and Planning A,* Vol. 33, pp. 79–95.

Yao, Shujie. 1996. "Sectoral Cointegration, Structural Break and Agriculture's Role in the Chinese Economy in 1952–92: A VAR Approach," *Applied Economics,* Vol. 28, pp. 1269–1279.

Yi Gang. 1994. *Money, Banking, and Financial Markets in China,* Westview Press, Boulder, Colo.

Yu Dechang. 1989. "A Preliminary Discussion of Surplus Agricultural Labor and Its Transfer Pattern," *Zhongguo nongcun jingji* (China's Rural Economy), No. 2, pp. 36–41.

Yuan Gangming. 2000. "An Empirical Analysis of the Bad Debts of China's State-Owned Enterprises," *Jingji yanjiu* (Economic Research), No. 5, pp. 12–20.

Zeng Peiyen, ed. 1999. *Xin zhongguo jingji wuxi nian, 1949–1999* (New China's Economy in the Last Fifty Years, 1949–1999), China Planning Press, Beijing.

Zhang Chunyuan, ed. 1991. *Zhongguo laonian renkou yanjiu* (Studies in China's Aged Population), Beijing University Press, Beijing.

Zhang, Shougong. 1999. *Catastrophic Flood Disaster in 1998 and the Post Factum Ecological and Environmental Reconstruction in China*, Harvard University Asia Center, www.fas.harvard.edu/~asiactr/fs_zhang2.htm.

Zhao Lukuan et al. 1998. *Laodong jiuye yu laodongli shichang jianshe* (Employment and the Building of Labor Markets), Jiangsu People's Press, Nanjing.

Zhao Renwei, and K. Griffin, eds. 1994. *Zhongguo jumin shouru fengpei yanjiu* (Studies in the Distribution of Personal Income in China), China Social Sciences Press, Beijing.

Zhao Yi, ed. 2001. *Zhongguo guoyao shangye yinhang bulian zhizhan de xingzheng yu chuzhi* (The Formation and Handling of Nonperforming Assets in China's State Commercial Banks), China Price Press, Beijing.

Zheng Haihan, ed. 1998. *Guoyao qiye kuixuan yanjiu* (A Study of the Losses of State-Owned Enterprises), Economic Management Press, Beijing.

Zhou Xiaochuan and Zhu Li. 1987. "China's Banking System: Current Status, Perspective on Reform," *Journal of Comparative Economics*, No. 11, pp. 399–409.

Zhu Fenqi, Kao Tianhong, Qiu Tianjao, and Yang Qing. 1996. *Zhongguo fanpinkuen yanjiu* (A Study of China's Alleviation of Poverty), China Planning Press, Beijing.

Zhu Ling and Jiang Zhongyi. 1994. *Yikongdaizhun yu huanjie pinkuan* (Work-for-Relief and Poverty Alleviation), Shanghai People's Press, Shanghai.

Zhu Xiangdong. 2000. "The Twenty-First Century: Which Road to Alleviate Poverty?" *Xinhua yuehbao* (New China Monthly), No. 10, pp. 84–85.

Charles Wolf, Jr., is senior economic adviser and corporate fellow in international economics at RAND. Dr. Wolf is the former Dean of the RAND Graduate School and a senior research fellow at the Hoover Institution.

K. C. Yeh is a long-time authority on China's economy. Dr. Yeh is a former RAND senior staff member and currently a RAND consultant.

Benjamin Zycher is a senior economist at RAND. Dr. Zycher is also an adjunct scholar at the Cato Institute in Washington, a senior fellow at the Pacific Research Institute, and an adjunct fellow at the Claremont Institute.

Nicholas N. Eberstadt holds the Henry Wendt Chair in Political Economy at the American Enterprise Institute. Dr. Eberstadt is a visiting fellow at the Harvard Center for Population and Development Studies and senior research associate at The National Bureau of Asian Research.

Sung-Ho Lee is a doctoral fellow in the RAND Graduate School.

Water resources (*continued*)
and regional disparities, 75–79,
76n
annually renewable
resources, 78t
availability by province, 77f
water withdrawals, 79t
Water shortages. *See* Water resources
Water transfer project, 89–90
See also Water resources
"Wealthier Is Healthier" (Pritchett),
68n
"Weighing Up Disability" (James), 44n
Wheeler, David, 93
Wilson, Barry, 161n
Wolf, Charles, Jr., 3, 6n, 102n, 103n,
146n, 149n, 155n
Working-age population, 14n
World Bank, 3, 14, 15n, 22, 23, 25, 84,
88, 139
World Capital Markets (Dobson),
142n, 149n
World Health Organization (WHO),
43, 44, 45, 48–49, 50t
World Resource Institute (WRI), 75
World Trade Organization (WTO), 97,
136, 147, 159
Wuhan, 19
Wu Jinglian, 128

Xinjiang, 17, 52
Xu Sulin, 19n
Xu Xiaobo, 134

Yang, Andrew, 161n
Yang, Hong, 75, 77, 82, 91, 92, 97
Yangtze River, 76, 85, 89
Yang Yiyong, 11n, 12n, 24n, 134, 135
Yan Yulong, 123
Yao, Shujie, 95
Yasheng Huang, 151n
Yellow (Huang) River, 76, 79, 89, 90
Yi Gang, 123
Yuan Gangming, 125, 131

Zehnder, Alexander, 75, 77, 82, 91, 92,
97
Zeng Peiyen, 15n
Zhai Zhenwu, 14
Zhang, Shougong, 86
Zhao Renwei, 15n
Zhao Yi, 125, 128, 129, 131
Zhejiang, 134
Zhou Zhengqing, 121
Zhu Rongji, 146n